SUMO

A Pocket Guide

SUMO

A Pocket Guide

REVISED EDITION

Revised and edited
by David Shapiro

CHARLES E. TUTTLE COMPANY
Rutland, Vermont & Tokyo, Japan

Published by the Charles E. Tuttle Company, Inc.
of Rutland, Vermont & Tokyo, Japan
with editorial offices at
2–6 Suido 1–chome, Bunkyo-ku, Tokyo 112

LCC Card No. 89–50474
ISBN 0–8048–2014–7

First edition, 1989
First revised edition, 1995
Second printing, 1998

Printed in Singapore

Contents

 # Foreword

In the surprisingly long history of English-language writing on sumo, two volumes stand out as truly seminal works in the field. One is a volume called *A Guide to Sumo* written by the late J.A. Sargent, first published in 1959 by the Charles E. Tuttle Publishing Company. Although there was much talk about revising this proud part of the Tuttle catalogue, it was finally decided to allow the book to go out of print several years ago. The book you are now holding in your hands was originally designed to take the place of that respected volume. What it lacked in its first incarnation, though, was the depth of research required to fill that bill.

When it came time to revise *Sumo: A Pocket Guide*, Tuttle approached me with the idea of a return to the original book design in mind. I think the changes and revisions we have made over the course of this project have brought us as close as possible to achieving that aim.

In working on the book, I kept two goals in mind. The first was to stay as true to the spirit of the original author's work as humanly possible. The second goal was to add, wherever possible, information that would increase the quality of the presentation of this marvelous aspect of Japanese culture that is ever so much more than just another sport. You will notice that I maintained the original format, which was actually based on the Sargent book. Chapters 2, 3, 4, 5, 6, 7, 8, 10, 11, and 12 were updated and corrected to bring them more in line with contemporary sumo writing and research. Chapters 1, 9, and 13 were substantially rewritten. Chapter 1, retitled "As Old as the Nation," was rewritten to reflect a more mainstream view of sumo history research. Chapter 9, "The Grand Champions," was rewritten in order to give the readers an even better understanding of just how remarkable this rank is, through a more organized approach to the subject matter and a more substantial introduction to some of the men who have held the rank. Finally, Chapter 13, "The Lure of Sumo," was rewritten not only to enhance the reader's understanding of sumo's fascination to foreigners but to help them understand its unique position in Japanese society. The three addenda, "Chanko-nabe Restaurants," "Addresses and Phone Numbers of Sumo Stables," and the "Glossary of Sumo Terms" have also been updated and revised to make them even more useful than before.

Along with the author's original sources, I turned to several Japanese-language references that I have found to be invaluable tools in pursuing my work in sumo. The first, *Osumo Jiten,* published by Sanseido Co., Ltd., was produced under the supervision of Yoshitaka Takahashi, a former chairman of the Yokozuna Promotion Council. This is an excellent all-around guide and I used it heavily as a reference source related to sumo history. *Ozumo Kansen Gaido* (1994 edition), published by Nihon Spotsu Shuppansha and edited by Kinjiro Kagaya, was used as a reference in the examination of overall records as well as of more contemporary topics like income and prize money.

I relied on four sources for information related to individual careers and records. The first is the recently published and excellent *Ozumo Rikishi Meikan* (Volume 1), published by Kyodo Tsushinsha and edited by Naofumi Mizuno and Toshiharu Kyosu. I also referred to another recent publication entitled *Showa-Heisei no Ninki Rikishi 100 Nin*, which was edited by Shotaro Funaki and published by Nihon Spotsu Shuppansha. Finally, in my discussions of two legendary yokozuna in Chapter 9, Futabayama and Taiho, I turned to Baseball Magazine-sha's remarkable series *Showa no Mei Yokozuna: Volume 1*, "Futabayama," and *Volume 2*, "Taiho," edited respectively by Tsuneo Ikeda and Ikuo Ikeda. Mention should also be made here of the invaluable assistance supplied by the staff of the Sumo Museum, located in the complex that plays host to sumo in Tokyo, the Ryogoku Kokugikan. These people have always been generous with their time and talent in answering a variety of questions over the years, and their input helped to make this a better book.

In the original edition, the author took great pains to find a happy medium between the use of Japanese terminology and English equivalents. This is part of an ongoing debate in the field of sumo coverage, and I have altered usage in the text to reflect the direction this debate is taking. Certain English equivalents are still acceptable; "ring" for *dohyo* and "referee" for *gyoji*, for example. Where these translations are acceptable they are used freely. The most noteworthy change from the original text is in the use of the English-language term "wrestler." If sumo was nothing more than a combative sport, the use of this term would be justifiable. However, as you read this book, I hope you will discover just how much more than a sport sumo really is. This is one reason why the Japanese term for today's practitioners of the game, *rikishi*, is used wherever possible. The men in sumo themselves hate to be referred to by the term "wrestler" and there is a solid trend in English-language coverage to make rikishi the standard. (More on this choice of terminology in Chapter 2.)

Finally, as the original author mentioned in the first edition, this is not meant to be a complete guide to sumo. As the term "pocket guide" implies, this book is meant to be a broad overview, offering a taste or general understanding of what sumo is all about. For regular coverage of all aspects of sumo, *Sumo World*, the world's only English-language magazine specializing in sumo, is the best source around.

With the advent of satellite broadcasting in Japan, English-language coverage of each day of every tournament is now available on a greater scale than ever before, complements of NHK, Japan's public broadcasting corporation. In North America and Europe, contact your local cable companies for further information on whether these broadcasts are available in your area.

One of the things I enjoy so much about sumo, besides the fact that it is one of the most exciting spectator sports around, is its depth. There is always more to know, always more to discover in its rituals, traditions, and history. And for those students of Japanese culture looking for a unique route to some serious insights into what the Japanese people are all about, you would be surprised by what you can find in a study of Japan's national sport. But whatever your reasons for wanting to take a closer look at sumo, I hope this book serves you as a solid first step in the direction of achieving a greater understanding of an athletic/cultural endeavor that is as remarkable as it is unique.

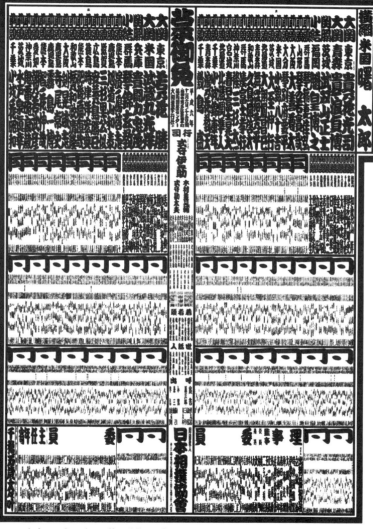

A *banzuke*, the official list of tournament participants.

CHAPTER 1

As Old as the Nation

Wrestling seems to have been around almost as long as a civilized mankind has. You can find it in most every culture in one form or another. The fact that there are only so many different ways in which you can grapple with an opponent guarantees that similar styles of wrestling will develop in completely unrelated cultures. This holds true for Japan's national sport, sumo, as well. You can find sumo-like sports in places as far apart as Egypt, Senegal, and Switzerland.

In Japan's case, the sport is as old as the nation itself, appearing in the country's creation mythology. This does not mean that it developed uninfluenced by outside forces. Japan's close ties to ancient China and the various kingdoms of what became known as the Korean peninsula ensured that there would be some impact of their versions of the sport on this country's brand of wrestling. However, sumo is generally considered to be one of the two truly indigenous aspects of Japanese culture, along with the Shinto religion to which it is closely tied. In fact, sumo finds its roots firmly planted in the soil of this ancient faith.

Shinto is an animistic religion closely tied to Japanese rice culture. It is filled with a pantheon of deities, and the Japanese imperial line traces its origins to the most powerful of them. Sumo as a religious function is referred to as *shinji-zumo* and it can still be found today as part of festival activities held at many Shinto shrines around the country. At the time of its origin, it was closely tied to the Japanese rice culture. Matches were performed at a local shrine to determine how good or bad a given harvest would be. As the national polity began to take shape under the suzerainty, or overlordship, of the imperial household, these matches were performed before the ruling emperor or empress to determine the outcome of the country's harvest, thus making *shinji-zumo* an event of national importance. By the Nara period (646–794) this had become an annual court event.

The next incarnation in sumo's long journey to what it has become today took place during the Heian period (794–1185). While it was still being practiced primarily as a religious service related to the rice harvest and, by this time, as an offering to the gods to obtain their protection of the nation, it was also performed as a court entertainment called *sumai no sechie*. This new usage of sumo as entertainment was an important step toward it becoming a sport.

These events were held to mark the changes of season and became national affairs with scouts being sent out across the land to find the most powerful competitors the country had to offer. Many of the best wrestlers of the day were farmers by trade. Since these court-organized competitions were held at some of the busiest times of the year down on the farm, it was not uncommon for a competitor to enter the capital city of Kyoto hog-tied and at swordpoint. In spite of this press-gang approach to recruiting, sumo's ties to the highly formalized lifestyle of the Heian court, coupled with its religious origins, would lead it to develop into a sport steeped in ritual.

The passing of the Heian period saw an end to the political control of the nation by the imperial court and, as such, its influence on the development of sumo. The Kamakura period (1185–1336) saw the beginning of the rule of the samurai, who embraced sumo with enthusiasm. To them, it was a perfect form of hand-to-hand combat as well as an excellent training tool. They did not ignore sumo's entertainment value though, and regularly held competitions as a way of passing the time between battles.

The loss of political influence by the imperial court also led to an equal decline in its wealth. One of the things that suffered as a result of this was the court's ability to hold spectacular ceremonial events on a grand scale, including sumai no sechie. Although shinji-zumo events were still being held at the grassroots level and the samurai were also practicing sumo on a regular basis, this turn of events led to a three hundred-odd year slump for sumo on the national stage. It was still a part of Japanese life, but no one was holding sumo tournaments with the same kind of national significance as those held by the Heian court.

All this was to change with the rise to power of the first

great shogun, Oda Nobunaga. A rough-and-tumble kind of guy who climbed up the ranks from fairly humble beginnings, Nobunaga liked his entertainment on the working-class side. One of his favorite pastimes was, naturally, sumo. In 1578 he gathered fifteen hundred men from across the land for a major one-day sumo competition. Sumo was once again a national pastime with what was to become regular performances before the powers that be.

During that protracted downturn in sumo's fortunes as a government-supported entity, it was evolving once again, this time on the local level. It was then, during the Muromachi period (1336–1568), that sumo took one more major step toward becoming a professional sport with the development of something called *kanjin-zumo*. These events involved bouts designed to raise money for improvements or repairs to the many temples and shrines that dotted the nation. The Muromachi period also saw the beginnings of professional sumo wrestlers, masterless samurai who banded together into troupes wandering the countryside to participate in kanjin-zumo events. These groups would usually receive a percentage of the gate and there was always cash and prizes available for the top competitors.

By the Tokugawa period (1603–1868), kanjin-zumo was becoming more professional and less charitable. This 268-year period, known in some sources as "The Pax Tokugawa," brought more than two centuries of peace and prosperity to the nation. With the rise of Ieyasu, the first Tokugawa shogun, the constant warring between various feudal lords was put to an end. As a result, even more warriors found themselves out of work, expanding the ranks of the wandering professional wrestlers.

This peace also led to the rise of a wealthy merchant class with money to burn and on the lookout for entertainment. Sumo fit the bill, and kanjin-zumo became less a means of raising money to repair important religious structures and more a means of lining the pockets of the participants. It reached the stage where a form of pickup bout called *tsuji-zumo*, or "street corner sumo," became popular. These were strictly cash bouts held wherever there was open ground. Gambling was rampant and the events often degenerated into brawls and sword fights.

Unable to control the problems surrounding these unauthorized competitions, the shogunate briefly banned both tsuji-zumo and kanjin-zumo in 1648 and again in 1661, the second ban lasting for over fifteen years. But by that time sumo's popularity was something that could not be denied, and in 1684 one of the founding fathers of organized professional sumo, Ikazuchi Gondaiyu, received permission from the government to put on a sumo tournament. Well structured and peaceful, it was a rousing success, and professional sumo was off and running.

Another interesting aspect of this extended period of political stability is the fact that Japan's feudal lords, under the watchful eye of the Tokugawa clan, had been forced to give up their right to pick fights with each other on a regular basis, and so turned to sumo patronage in a big way as an outlet, vicarious of course, for their aggressive and competitive urges. It was during this period that major administrative bodies developed in Tokyo, Osaka, and

Kyoto to control those regions' events. With the money available from both the feudal lords and the merchant class, these events became regular affairs. It was also during this period that sumo grew and developed into a form pretty close to what is seen today.

Given its ancient roots, sumo has naturally accrued a great deal of lore, legend, and a vast array of anecdotes involving the many characters that populate its history. The next chapter takes a look at a few of these individuals.

CHAPTER 2

Odds and Ends, Past and Present

The first recorded sumo bout was a rather straightforward affair, fought at the request of Emperor Suinin around 23 B.C. This fight pitted the formidable wrestler Taima-no-Kehaya against Nomi-no-Sukune, who supposedly stood 2.38 meters tall (seven feet ten inches). After a long, pitched battle that reportedly thrilled the audience, Sukune dealt Kehaya a powerful, well-placed kick that broke his ribs and killed him on the spot. The property of the loser was seized and given to Sukune, who was also awarded a position as a retainer of the emperor. This bout appears in the *Kojiki (Record of Ancient Matters)*, Japan's earliest written history, compiled around 712. Shrines to both of these early sumo wrestlers can be found in Western Japan in what was once known as the land of Yamato, the area ruled by Suinin and his descendants.

A thirteenth-century text chronicles an instance of the imperial succession being decided by the outcome of a sumo bout. When Emperor Montoku announced his intention to retire in 858, the throne was claimed by both his eldest son, Koretaka, and his fourth son, Korehito. The emperor decreed that the matter would be settled by a match, and men were chosen to represent each side. The eldest son was championed by a powerful-looking giant named Natora, while Korehito was represented by a scrawny little fellow named Yoshio. Unknown to all, however, the most important player in the drama was a Buddhist priest in a nearby temple who was praying fervently for a miracle.

As the bout opened, Yoshio was grabbed by his much bigger opponent and hurled into the air. To the spectators watching the match, it appeared that Natora had won without even trying, but Yoshio was able to land on his feet. Suddenly, in response to the priest's prayers, a huge water buffalo in a nearby rice paddy began to bellow. Before the much-larger Natora could attempt his next technique, the sound of the buffalo's cries seemed to sap his strength. Yoshio, seeing this, quickly went on the offensive and won the bout. Korehito became the emperor Seiwa, who went on to rule until 876.

Sumo wrestlers are, and in the main always have been, men. But there have been some interesting exceptions. Legend has it that at a benefit sumo tournament held in Kyoto in 594, victory seemed all but assured for a wrestler called Tateishi. After he had beaten all of his opponents, the referee stepped forward and called out to the crowd for more challengers. It appeared that no one was going to respond, when up stepped a young nun. Tateishi at first refused to fight, but the audience was so amused that he figured he would play along with the jest.

As the nun moved toward him, he simply stood with his arms spread. But when she began to actually push him backward, he became horrified and began to wrestle in earnest. When he crouched and grabbed for her arm, however, she took hold of his thigh and threw him to the ground. The crowd went wild. Tateishi was mortified, but his embarrassment was somewhat mitigated when the nun threw the next three challengers. The wrestling nun later appeared in several more tournaments, always winning.

In the Edo period, bouts were actually held between women. These were not really displays of combative skill but reflected the sport's growing role as a popular entertainment; the women's mud wrestling of its day. The wrestlers themselves were not much to look at, if contemporary prints are any reliable guide, and they had names as grotesque as their appearance, such as Chichigahari, or "Swollen Tits," and Anagafuchi, or "Deep Trench." For the crowd's amusement, the women were often matched against blind men, leading to much groping and grabbing.

On the more serious side, wrestlers have figured in some important political transitions, and not only of the legendary kind related above. A group of them participated in the taking of Shimonoseki during the Choshu Civil War of 1865. Their successful resistance against the forces of the Tokugawa shogunate helped to contribute to the eventual restoration to power of the Meiji emperor in 1868, an event that heralded Japan's drive to modernization.

Wrestlers are referred to by the term *rikishi* (literally "gentleman of strength"), which dates from the early eighteenth century. Another term, *sumotori*, or "someone who does sumo," is often used by the Japanese public in general. Sumotori, however, does not accurately express what being a professional participant in this sport is all about, and it is not the term used by the men themselves. Professional sumo's governing body also prefers the former term to the latter.

Whereas many rikishi once came from the ranks of unemployed samurai, today they are mostly the sons of farming or fishing families. Many hail from northern Japan, particularly the great island of Hokkaido. One reason for this, it has been suggested, is that trudging through the heavy snows that blanket northern Japan during the winter strengthens the hips and legs, which is something vital for success in sumo.

There may be some merit to this argument. To avoid being toppled, a rikishi's center of gravity should be as low as possible. A "natural" would then have relatively short legs with wide hips and well-developed thighs, as well as a thick upper torso. The weight and stability of his lower body make him difficult to move or throw, and that is a key to the sport. Life in Japan's "snow country" certainly produces such a physique. As for the great number of rikishi from Kyushu, Japan's relatively snowless southern main island, many of these men come from fishing families. Long hours on small boats hauling heavy nets will also help to create a physique perfect for sumo.

And then there is the foreign contingent. Japanese society has been described as being for the most part closed to foreigners. Until not long ago, the tightly knit world of sumo was even more so. In 1885, the request of an American to join the sport was refused. During World War

II, however, an American-born Japanese reached the top division in professional sumo's ranks. A few years after that, he was followed by a Japanese-born Korean named Rikidozan. Quite a colorful character, Rikidozan abruptly quit sumo in 1950. As one of his reasons for leaving, he charged that as a foreigner he was not allowed to advance to the rank of champion. However, it is likely that monetary difficulties subsequent to a prolonged illness played the biggest role in his decision to quit.

After his retirement, Rikidozan shocked the sumo world by going into professional wrestling. Although Japanese professional wrestling at the time was filled with former rikishi who never made it to the top two divisions, Rikidozan was the first former top division star to join the "grunt-and-groan circuit." He became quite popular and successful, however, and later retired to manage a number of nightclubs. He died tragically in 1963, stabbed to death by a gangster outside one of his clubs.

As Japan became more prosperous and international in its outlook, the world of sumo also opened up a bit. Koreans, Chinese, Brazilians, Tongans, and mainland Americans have all tried their hand at it. Most have given up and returned home, not due to any overt discrimination but simply because, as we shall see, the life of a novice wrestler is difficult for many to cope with. Some foreigners have achieved outstanding success, however, with a string of four Hawaiians taking turns rewriting the pages of sumo history.

The first of this quartet went by the ring name of Takamiyama. Today as a stablemaster, he goes by the name Azumazeki, and is better known as the man who coached another Hawaiian, Akebono, to sumo's highest rank. In his heyday, however, he was a real trailblazer, and it is safe to say that the recent successes of the Hawaiian contingent would have been a lot more difficult to achieve without him.

Born Jesse James Walani Kuhaulua, Jesse, as he is still popularly known, entered sumo in 1964 at the age of nineteen. Four years later he was fighting in sumo's top division, and four years after that he became the first foreigner ever to win a top division championship. During the awards presentation following his victory, the American ambassador to Japan read a congratulatory telegram from President Richard Nixon. An amiable bear of a man, Jesse was one of the most popular rikishi of his day.

This accomplishment in and of itself would have been enough to guarantee the former *sekiwake* (sumo's third highest rank) an important place in sumo history, but Jesse was also one of the true "iron men" of his sport, spending twenty years in sumo. His amazing durability resulted in several records: for the most tournaments in the top division, ninety-seven; for the most career bouts in the top division, 1,430; and the most consecutive appearances in the top division, 1,231. He is also ranked fourth on the list for top-division victories, with 683. What makes this achievement all the more impressive is the fact that the three rikishi ranked ahead of him are considered to be three of the greatest *yokozuna*, or "grand champions," who have ever lived. Jesse became a Japanese citizen in 1980 and opened his own stable two years after his retirement in 1984.

The second in this Hawaiian group, Konishiki, was

recruited by Jesse for his old stable, Takasago, and entered professional sumo in 1982. He raced up the ranks in dramatic fashion, reaching the top division in 1984. Three years later, after the 1987 May Grand Sumo Tournament, Konishiki was promoted to sumo's second highest rank, *ozeki*, becoming the first foreigner to gain this honor. He successfully defended the rank for thirty-nine consecutive tournaments, taking third place on the all-time list in this category. During that period, he won the top division title three times. He also has the dubious honor of being the heaviest man in sumo history, weighing a whopping 269 kilograms (591 pounds).

The third and fourth Hawaiian-born rikishi, Akebono and Musashimaru, have put themselves in the position of leading professional sumo into the twenty-first century. When Akebono, or Chad Rowan, entered the professional ranks in 1988, most of the experts felt that although his size was impressive, his hips were much too high for him to achieve any kind of success in the sport. He proved the experts wrong, and in January of 1993, after winning two consecutive top-division titles ranked at ozeki, was promoted to become the sixty-fourth yokozuna, marking the first time a foreigner would hold sumo's highest rank. To date he has won seven top-division championships and, following successful arthroscopic surgery on both knees, is expected to play a dominant role in sumo for many years to come.

Musashimaru, like his three fellow Hawaiians, has also been working hard to rewrite the record books. In the six years since his professional debut in September 1989, he has gotten as far as ozeki, winning his first top-division title in July 1994 with a perfect 15–0 record, only one of fifteen men to achieve this feat in the modern era.

From wherever they hail, aspiring rikishi must be of a minimum height and weight. These standards have been raised gradually over the years, as improvement in the Japanese diet has produced successively taller and more massive competitors. Today, young men who desire to join sumo must stand at least 1.73 meters (five feet eight inches) and weigh at least seventy-five kilograms (165 pounds).

Considering the size of the top-ranked rikishi, these standards seem very minimum indeed. For even taking into account legendary giants, the biggest men in sumo history are those wrestling today, with the top-division average weight now 157 kilograms (346 pounds). Obviously, then, most of the rikishi's bulk results from the diet and training regimen that he undertakes after entering sumo. These and other aspects of the newcomer's long and difficult struggle to the top are the subjects of Chapters 3 and 4.

CHAPTER 3

The Long Climb

A new recruit enters sumo by becoming affiliated with a training facility called a *heya*, a term commonly translated as "stable." Many heya are located near Tokyo's Ryogoku Station on the JR Sobu Line, for it was in this area that the first national sumo stadium, the Kokugikan, was constructed in 1909. There are about a dozen heya clustered around the newest Kokugikan, which opened in 1985 in the same vicinity, and almost fifty altogether (a list of heya addresses and phone numbers appears on pages 95–99). Most heya are relatively simple structures; ordinary wood-frame or concrete houses, each containing little more than a ring, a communal eatery, and some rather spartan living quarters. In keeping with Japan's overall prosperity though, there is a trend today toward building more impressive structures, with a sophisticated weight-training room being the most common addition.

The young hopeful must pass a physical examination,

held six times a year (before each of the major tournaments), and must present the required documents (proof of junior high school graduation, parental consent, and a copy of the family register). He is then formally enrolled as an apprentice and is guaranteed nothing more than a roof, three square meals, long hours of hard work, and a chance at stardom. The newcomer might be a strapping farm boy or fisherman's son with little training in the sport, or a veteran college wrestler. But in any case, he has a long and difficult climb ahead of him.

These stables house a total of over 850 rikishi and all are competing in the struggle upward through a rigid system of ranks. Ascending through the sumo hierarchy is somewhat like climbing a mountain. Progress can be rather quick and painless at its broad-based entry level, but it becomes progressively more difficult as one approaches the steep and slippery summit. As a matter of fact, the word *nobori*, "to climb," is a popular suffix for a rikishi's ring name; it gives notice of his intention to climb to the summit of the sumo world.

There are six major divisions in sumo. These are best considered as forming a figurative mountain divided into two main groups. Its base is subdivided into four groups and its summit consists of two groups, with a wide disparity in the prestige and privileges accorded members of the bottom four and the top two. The four lower divisions are (from the bottom up): the Jonokuchi division, with about one hundred rikishi; the Jonidan division, with about three hundred; the Sandanme division, with about two hundred; and the Makushita division, fixed at 120 rikishi.

Although the numbers in the divisions below Makushita vary, a little arithmetic reveals that this leaves only sixty-odd slots in the top two divisions—a precipitous summit indeed.

A novice, as a matter of fact, does not really begin to climb the mountain right away; he is only allowed to view it from a distance as he hikes towards it. For although he is officially a member of the sumo world, the bouts in his first tournament are considered *mae-zumo* (literally "pre-sumo") and his name will not appear on the *banzuke*, or "official list" of tournament rankings.

Mae-zumo bouts are held early in the morning during grand sumo tournaments. In the old days, the novice needed three wins to graduate from mae-zumo. Today, win, lose, or draw he will wind up ranked in the lowest division, Jonokuchi, for the next tournament. His three-match record will decide just how high or low in that division he will sit. Following the completion of his three bouts, he will make his first formal appearance before the public in a special ceremony held in the ring during this debut tournament.

There is one exception to this procedure. Experienced college wrestlers who have won or placed highly in certain designated amateur tournaments are allowed to compete from the bottom of the Makushita division, bypassing mae-zumo and the lowest ranks.

The first of our two divisions at the top of the mountain is the Juyro division. This is topped by the highest, the Makunouchi division. The former takes its name from an old Japanese coin called a *ryo*. Ten ryo, or *juryo*, was the salary of a rikishi in that division. The Juyro division has twenty-six rikishi; Makunouchi has approximately thirty-eight to forty.

Rikishi in these top two divisions are referred to as *sekitori*, meaning "to capture the barrier." This term dates from Japan's middle ages, when a wrestler who had defeated all his opponents was said to have "taken the barrier." It later came to mean a truly powerful wrestler. Becoming a sekitori brings with it a huge leap in status. More than any other promotion, save perhaps to ozeki or yokozuna, it is the mark of success in a sumo career.

Sekitori status is readily evident from a rikishi's apparel and hairstyle. All rikishi let their hair grow when they enter sumo. When it grows long enough it is first tied in a simple topknot called a *chonmage*, and is kept in place with a scented pomade called *bintsuke abura*. For tournaments and other formal occasions, sekitori sport a more elaborate *ichomage* (or *o-icho*) hairstyle, where the hair is pulled back, gathered and then fanned out in the shape of a gingko leaf.

Rank can also be determined from the quality of the belt, or *mawashi*, a rikishi wears when he competes. It is made from about nine meters (thirty feet) of cloth, folded lengthwise a number of times, passed between the legs, and then wrapped around the waist. Rikishi practice in a mawashi of cotton canvas, black for the lower divisions and white for sekitori. For tournaments, sekitori switch to mawashi of pure silk, often in bright colors, while lower-division rikishi must make do with their practice mawashi. During tournaments, all rikishi wear tucked into the front of their mawashi a thin band of cords called a *sagari*, made of cotton for the lower ranks and starched silk for the sekitori. These are symbolic athletic supporters that indicate that it is illegal to grab the area they hang over.

Sumo may be rigidly structured but it is eminently fair. Advancement through the ranks comes through winning tournament bouts, and thus depends entirely on the individual. Following each tournament, rikishi are re-ranked on the basis of their performance. Since sumo has no weight classes, this method ensures that rikishi will for the most part be matched against opponents of similar power and ability. Achieving a majority of wins, or *kachi-koshi,* means promotion; a rikishi who records more losses than wins, or *make-koshi,* will be demoted. The degree of promotion or demotion is in proportion to the rikishi's win-loss record as well as the records of those around him.

Rikishi do not wrestle more than once a day during tournaments. Those in the lower ranks participate in only seven bouts, while sekitori fight in fifteen. With only seven bouts per tournament, it takes time for a lower-ranking rikishi to work his way up to the top two divisions; six to seven years has been considered average. However, since there are more grand tournaments now than there were in the past, and since college wrestlers bypass the lowest divisions, it is now possible to advance through the ranks with greater speed. About a half-dozen of the top sekitori now wrestling won promotion to the Makunouchi division within two years of entering sumo. But these are exceptions, and there are several who took more than ten years.

Makunouchi means "inside the curtain," from the days when wrestlers sat in a curtained area awaiting their bouts.

The thirty-eight-odd rikishi in this division are further divided into several ranks. At the bottom are the *maegashira* (literally "before the head"), who are ranked by number, from maegashira one, the highest, through a maximum of sixteen. Two rikishi share each designation, one representing the position for the east, one for the west. As with much of sumo culture, this traditional division dates from ancient times, and now serves as a convenient method of organizing rankings and tournament bouts, with an east ranking considered slightly higher than a ranking on the west.

The difficulty of becoming a member of the elite Makunouchi group is readily evident from the numbers: the division's rikishi total, after all, represents less than five percent of all competitors active in the sport. Moreover, not even a Makunouchi division rikishi can rest on his laurels. Since his rank is reevaluated after each tournament, he will bounce up and down within, or even in and out of, the division. It often happens that a rikishi, after a particularly successful tournament, wins promotion to a high ranking that is really beyond his capabilities. Meeting mostly top men in the next tournament, he compiles a dismal record, which sends him down into the ranks of men not as capable. So he trounces them all in the next tournament and shoots to the top again. Such men are popularly referred to as "elevator rikishi."

Above the maegashira are the *sanyaku*, the three ranks of ordinary titleholders. The highest of these is ozeki, or "champion," followed by the *sekiwake*, sometimes translated as "junior champion" and finally the *komusubi*, or "junior champion, second grade." There are usually two each of the sekiwake and komusubi, one each on the east and west sides, and anywhere from one to four ozeki.

The two lower-grade title holders are subject to the same rules for promotion and demotion as the other rikishi, but the ozeki are given a break. They will not be demoted unless they fail to make kachi-koshi in two successive tournaments. Ozeki literally means "great barrier," which in the sumo world it truly is; only about one in five hundred attain this rank.

Finally, above the sanyaku are the yokozuna, or "grand champions," who stand at the pinnacle of sumo. Subject neither to promotion nor demotion, yokozuna are in a class—and hence a chapter—by themselves.

CHAPTER 4

Life in the Stables

Although feudalism supposedly came to an end in Japan in 1868, some say it is alive and thriving in the sumo stable. Having sworn fealty to his new lord, the stablemaster, the aspiring rikishi does whatever he is told to do. As a trainee he will be asked to work as a cook, janitor, and *tsukebito*, or "personal manservant," to a sekitori or coach. He will take on the dirtiest and most menial chores of the heya, in return for which he will receive only the necessities of life and the chance to advance. Meanwhile, he will take his place at the bottom of a rigid hierarchy, first whenever there is work to be done and last whenever it is time to eat or relax. Warm-up exercises and practice in the stable are also undertaken in order of rank, lowest to highest. Novices must rise early, around half-past five, to get started with their workouts, while the senior rikishi sleep in until a more reasonable hour. There is no breakfast, no eating or drinking of any kind, before practice.

New recruits also go back to school, this time under the tutelage of the Japan Sumo Association. Located in the Kokugikan, the school curriculum includes a grueling daily workout where the recruits learn the basic techniques, including how to fall safely. They also study the history and traditions of sumo and practice enough calligraphy to be able to sign an elegant autograph. After six months of this basic indoctrination, the newcomers will have acquired enough knowledge to handle themselves in sumo society and enough skill to enable them to train with their senior stablemates.

Many of sumo's basic exercises and training routines are unique to the sport. Rikishi practice a variety of movements designed to stretch and loosen the muscles; the two basic exercises are called *shiko* and *matawari*. The former is performed by lifting a leg straight up to the side, as high as possible, then slamming the foot to the ground. The hard thumping has a symbolic significance and figures prominently in the pre-bout ceremony at tournaments; here its purpose is to loosen and strengthen the muscles and joints of the hips and legs. Matawari is sometimes translated as "sumo splits." Seated on the ground with each leg extended as straight out to the side as possible, the rikishi bends over until his upper chest and shoulders touch the ground. The younger rikishi often cannot attain this painful-looking position and are helped by their seniors who push down on their backs.

Another exercise certainly found only in sumo is *teppo*, the slapping of a wooden pillar with the open hands, one after the other. This is performed in conjunction with sweeping foot motions to help coordinate arm and leg

movement. Shiko and teppo are normally performed before practice bouts; matawari is performed after.

Training of all types is referred to as *keiko* (pronounced
"geiko" as a suffix). The first keiko of the day is usually
moshiai-geiko, a kind of "king of the mountain" played in
the practice ring. Two rikishi square off and fight, with the
winner choosing the next challenger. Obviously, the more
you win the more practice you get and, theoretically at
least, the stronger you get. All of the training is carefully
watched by the stable coaches and, perhaps, the
stablemaster himself. A rikishi not displaying the proper
enthusiasm or energy will find his instruction punctuated
with the sharp rap of a broom handle or bamboo sword.

Each level of practice concludes with a session of *butsu-
kari-geiko.* This involves one rikishi charging across the
ring, or *dohyo,* and trying to push out his opponent, who is
well braced for the attack. The exercise is repeated by the
same two rikishi until the attacker is covered in sand and
sweat, exhausted to the point where he is unable to stand.
As the morning practice continues, rikishi of progressively
higher divisions take their turns in the ring and then move
off to perform their winding-down exercises elsewhere,
followed usually by chores. Around eight o'clock or so, the
sekitori make their appearance. They begin their training
bouts around nine, when the younger rikishi return to
watch and assist.

One other common form of training, and one favored
by the sekitori, is called *sanban-geiko.* This consists of the
same two men fighting successive bouts; it is both a test of
endurance and a chance to hone technical skills. Sanban-
geiko also often takes place between rikishi of different

divisions, and thus provides an excellent training opportunity for the lower-ranked men. Higher-ranked rikishi try at all times to help out their juniors. The assistance may be in the form of a little extra instruction in technique, training methods, or in how to fight a particular opponent.

Training concludes before noon, usually with exercises and a short period of meditation. Before tournaments, rikishi often train with rikishi from a neighboring stable. Called *de-geiko*, or "outside training," it allows rikishi to engage in practice bouts with opponents they may actually meet in competition. While the sekitori are practicing, the first and main meal of the day is being prepared in the kitchen by the junior rikishi. Before eating, the sekitori file off to their baths, which also have been prepared by the juniors. The tsukebito scrub down the backs of their assigned seniors, who then head off to lunch. Since everything in sumo is decided by rank, juniors are always last in the bath and last to eat.

The main dish at the meal is the famous *chanko-nabe*, a stew consisting of some type of meat or fish cooked with a variety of vegetables in a broth. Spinach, leeks, carrots, daikon (a large, long white radish), Chinese cabbage, and Japanese mushrooms are a few of the vegetables used, and tofu is usually added. Eaten with several side dishes, many bowls of white rice and washed down with beer or saké, this high protein, high carbohydrate meal is calculated to put on weight, especially when followed by a mandatory nap of several hours.

Afternoons at the stable are fairly quiet. Married sekitori usually leave after the noon meal, while the junior rikishi still have many errands to run elsewhere. Unmarried sekitori will usually return to their private rooms. Everyone else lives communally, where they may simply rest before evening social obligations. As with other heroes in the public eye, the senior rikishi are in great demand to appear for worthy civic or charitable causes, as well as to promote business ventures. In addition, they must satisfy the demands of their fans and supporters. While the sekitori are out being wined and dined, the junior rikishi have their evening meal in the heya, usually a simple affair.

As noted in the previous chapter, a quantum leap in privilege and prestige comes with the attainment of sekitori status. Promotion to the Juryo division marks an end to a rikishi's service to others; in the future, he will be served. He will be assigned a tsukebito, who will run errands for him, answer his phone, and assist him in bathing and dressing. He may now get married and live away from the stable, and, while he remains a bachelor, he will be given a private room. The new sekitori must also be supplied with the accouterments befitting his new status. He will need the elaborately embroidered apron called a *kesho-mawashi,* which is worn during the ring-entering ceremony performed before the day's action in the top two divisions.

The kesho-mawashi is usually presented by the stable's *koenkai,* or "supporters club." Another may be presented later by the new sekitori's own koenkai, which he is now entitled to have. The sekitori will be given a new mawashi of silk, for use in tournaments, and a lacquered wickerware trunk called an *akeni,* in which his tsukebito will carry all this new equipment. All in all, life for the new sekitori will become more pleasant, although in truth he will have more work to do, for he will now wrestle on all fifteen days of the tournament, and the level of competition he will face will be much higher. On the other hand, he will finally get paid for his work: only sekitori receive regular salaries.

CHAPTER 5

Grand Sumo Tournaments

Unlike many other sports, sumo does not have a season. It takes place throughout the year, and there is no regular competition that culminates in a post-season championship contest like a Super Bowl or World Series. Perhaps it would be more accurate to say that each of the six fifteen-day sumo tournaments held each year is a complete season in itself, for in each a series of bouts culminates in the matching of rikishi with the best records, one of whom will be declared a particular division's tournament champion.

Sumo tournaments are called *basho,* meaning "place" or "site," a word that is added as a suffix to seasons or locations to form the name of a given tournament. As we have seen, by the middle of the seventeenth century the sport had become quite popular throughout the country and tournaments were being held regularly. They took place outdoors in specially constructed arenas on the grounds of shrines or temples. Patrons could sit on mats in roped-off boxes at the ground level, or in tiered balconies that could be reached by bamboo ladders.

These complexes were surrounded by high wooden walls to keep out freeloaders, and tea houses were set up nearby to cater to the patrons. About this time, the list of tournament contenders, the banzuke, began to take on its modern form. The single-sheet, vertical banzuke that we know today dates from the mid-eighteenth century and was developed in Edo (today's Tokyo) in competition with the horizontal design popular in western Japan at the time. A later refinement was the listing of rikishi in progressively larger characters as their rank increased. This had two obvious advantages: status-conscious Japanese could see at a glance who were the top rikishi, and the names of lower-ranked competitors—who were far more numerous than those in the upper ranks— could all be squeezed onto a single page. This format is almost identical to the one used today. Incidentally, banzuke make handy and inexpensive souvenirs. As of this writing, they can be purchased for the low price of ¥50 each (about U.S. 50¢) at the offices of the Japan Sumo Association in the Kokugikan beginning thirteen days prior to all basho.

Sumo remained a biannual event in Tokyo throughout the Meiji and Taisho periods (1868–1926), though up to 1925 there was a separate sumo organization operating in Osaka. Additional basho were added in the 1940s and 1950s in response to the sport's increasing popularity and the desire of fans in other parts of Japan to see it live. In 1953, an Osaka tournament and a third Tokyo tournament were officially added. In 1957 another tournament was established in the city of Fukuoka, located on Japan's southern island of Kyushu, and, finally, a basho in Nagoya was added in 1958.

Today, the annual sumo schedule starts with the Hatsu Basho, or "New Year's Tournament," held in January in Tokyo. The Haru Basho (Spring Tournament) is held in Osaka in March, after which Tokyo is again the host for the Natsu Basho (Summer Tournament) held in May. The Nagoya Basho is held in July, followed by the Aki Basho (Autumn Tournament) in Tokyo in September. The Kyushu Basho held in November is the last tournament of the year. One can gather two facts from this schedule: the first is that Tokyo is still very much the center of the sumo world, and the second is that, with important bouts on ninety days of the year, rikishi must be a very hardy lot indeed.

Common venues for sumo in the early Edo days were the Eiko-in Temple in Ryogoku and Asakusa Kuramae Hachiman Shrine, both located in the old entertainment quarters of the city. The largest of the outdoor arenas could hold more than three thousand people, a sizable number at the time but too small to satisfy the growing legions of fans. Sumo's popularity continued to increase until finally, in 1909, the first Kokugikan, with a seating capacity of 13,000, was built in Ryogoku. Kokugikan literally means "National Sport Hall," that is, a stadium for the national sport, sumo. The naming of the new hall marked the first time such a claim for the sport had been publicly made. The Kokugikan burned to the ground in 1917, was rebuilt, then destroyed again in 1923 during the Great Kanto Earthquake. It was rebuilt again, only to be severely damaged in the air raids that pummeled Tokyo during World War II.

For most of the Occupation, the stadium was unavailable for sumo, having been renamed Memorial Hall and used in part as an ice-skating rink for American soldiers. However, sumo thrived again in outdoor venues, and in 1950 construction of a new Kokugikan was begun up the road from Ryogoku in a place called Kuramae. Tournaments were held there even before the building was completed. The Kuramae Kokugikan served as the home of sumo until 1985, when the present Ryogoku Kokugikan was opened. Seating over 11,000 and built at a cost of U.S. $60 million, the spacious new stadium also houses the sumo training school, a clinic, the sumo museum, and the offices of the Japan Sumo Association.

That Japan is expensive is a common complaint, but for the real sumo fan a day at the Kokugikan is a bargain. Holding the cheapest ticket (as of this writing, ¥2,300 for an advance ticket, about U.S. $23), the sumo aficionado can settle into a seat around half past nine in the morning and watch the action until just before six in the evening. This price is for a seat in the last reserved row, however, with the present popularity of the sport, even these tickets are hard to come by. It is a common practice, among both Japanese and foreign fans, to sit in someone else's better, more expensive seat until he or she arrives (this is being reported, not recommended). Of course, there are more expensive ways to go. A party of four in a fairly good box will typically spend about U.S. $150 apiece for the day, including food and drinks.

Aside from the competition, a day at sumo can be quite

interesting, for it has its own emotional rhythm and one unconsciously absorbs the feeling of the building excitement and suspense. The bouts are held in order of rank, with the junior rikishi fighting early in the day, those in one division followed by those of the next higher up. There is a casualness about the morning's proceedings on the part of the spectators. Most of the seats are empty and there is a lot of talking and walking around. Throughout the early afternoon, the seats continue to fill. More attention is paid to the bouts and the background noise level rises, occasionally to be punctuated by shouts of encouragement to a favored competitor. Beer, saké, and *obento* (Japanese box lunches) appear, and the crowd eats, drinks, and becomes a little merrier.

The first of the afternoon's many climaxes occurs around three o'clock, with the *dohyo-iri*, or "ring-entering ceremony," of the Juryo division rikishi. This ceremony will be covered in more detail in the next chapter. Here, let it be said that it is quite spectacular and, for the first time in the day, commands the rapt attention of the entire audience. More important, it signals the beginning of the sekitori bouts, the competition between rikishi in the top two divisions. Also around this time, television coverage begins. The cameras require bright lights and when these come on, the crowd for some reason gets livelier and noisier. Perhaps those of the TV generation feel that video coverage brings with it the sanction of importance.

After the Juryo bouts, the rikishi of the top division ranked below yokozuna arrive and perform their dohyo-iri, followed by the yokozuna and theirs. This heralds the beginning of the Makunouchi bouts, which will culminate in those of the grand champions. By this time the atmosphere is charged. The slightest gesture on the dohyo brings a reaction from the crowd, and a skillful win brings thunderous applause. But before getting into the actual competition, the next chapter will examine briefly some of the tradition infusing what spectators see happening before them.

CHAPTER 6

Pageantry, Ritual, and Symbol

Go to a Japanese wedding, attend any traditional musical or theatrical performance, or join in one of the thousands of local festivals held throughout the year and one will likely sense the Japanese love of pageantry, ritual, and symbol. Not only are these important in religious practice, where one would normally expect to find them, but they seem to permeate business, entertainment, and sport. Sumo is no exception. With its ties to the Shinto religion and its early function as an imperial entertainment, one would expect to find it filled with colorful pageantry, ritual gestures, and symbolic trappings. And one is not disappointed. Ritual and pageantry are at no time more evident than during the dohyo-iri, the ring-entering ceremony performed by the rikishi in the top two divisions, Juryo and Makunouchi.

The two sides, east and west, perform their ceremonies separately. Preceded by a referee, the rikishi march single file into the arena in order of rank, lowest first, dressed in their colorful kesho-mawashi. These are beautiful, elaborately embroidered aprons, usually donated by a rikishi's koen-kai and costing ¥800,000 (U.S. $8,000) and up. Popular rikishi may have one for each day of the tournament.

As their names are called out by an announcer, the rikishi mount the dohyo and form a circle, facing outward toward the audience. After the last has arrived, the rikishi turn inward to face each other and perform a ritual that includes clapping, raising their arms into the air, and hiking up their kesho-mawashi an inch or two. Each of these movements has significance: the clapping announces to the gods that someone pure is asking for their attention and favor; the raising of the hands indicates that no weapons are being carried or concealed; and the hoisting of aprons is symbolic of the ritual foot-stamping that precedes a bout. The rikishi then depart as they entered. This ceremony is performed four times, by the east and west sides of the top two divisions, each day of the tournament.

The ring-entering ceremony for a yokozuna is, as one would expect, somewhat more elaborate. Led into the arena by the chief referee, a grand champion is also preceded by an attendant who serves as an usher, called a *tsuyu-harai* (literally "dew-sweeper"). The yokozuna is followed by his *tachi-mochi*, or "sword bearer." These positions are filled by maegashira-ranked rikishi from the yokozuna's stable or a related stable if men of sufficiently high rank are not available at home. Over his kesho-mawashi, the grand champion wears his *tsuna*, a thick, white rope that is the emblem of his rank. From it are hung *gohei*, zigzag white paper strips that are used in the Shinto religion to mark a sacred object or area. On the dohyo, the grand champion runs through a complex series of gestures while his attendants squat on either side. In addition to raising his arms and clapping, the ritual of the yokozuna includes several shiko, the hoisting of a leg high into the air before slamming it to the ground. This gesture, intended to frighten away malignant spirits, is also said to demonstrate the grand champion's intention to crush all opponents.

There are actually two traditional types of yokozuna dohyo-iri: the *unryu* and *shiranui* styles, named after the Edo-period yokozuna who supposedly performed them. The former was handed down from Unryu Hisakichi (1823–91), the tenth yokozuna; the latter was favored by Shiranui Koemon (1825–79), the eleventh. The unryu style combines both an offensive and defensive posture, while the shiranui style symbolizes an all-out offense. The two differ in the position of the hands following the first set of shiko in the center of the ring, as well as in the shape of the large knot at the back of the tsuna.

The dohyo itself is constructed of a special dirt called *rakida*, often obtained from Tokyo's neighboring Chiba Prefecture. The dohyo is .6 meters (two feet) high and 5.5 meters (eighteen feet) square at the base, and its surface is covered with a thin layer of sand. Embedded in it are straw bales called *tawara*, forming a circle 4.6 meters (fifteen feet) in diameter. The word dohyo is actually a compound of *do*, a variant reading of the character for "earth," and *hyo*, a variant of the character for "bale." Two of the bales

Musashigawa stable's Musashimaru, one of the Hawaiian-born rikishi competing in the professional ranks, became the first foreigner to win the top division title with a perfect 15–0 record in July of 1994 (*right*). His giant fellow countryman Konishiki spent a good part of his career at sumo's second-highest rank of ozeki, and won the top division title three times (*below*).

Hazing, intended to instill fighting spirit, is an accepted part of sumo stable life.

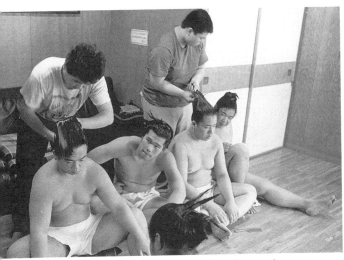

Rikishi have their hair attended to (*above*) and enjoy the
one-pot meal called *chanko-nabe* (*below*).

Tokyo tournaments are held at the Kokugikan, which opened in 1985.

By the time the higher-ranked rikishi are ready to meet, the 11,000-plus seat Kokugikan is filled to capacity.

One of the high points of the spectacle that is sumo is the *dohyo-iri* or "ring-entering ceremony" of the rikishi competing in the top two divisions. The rikishi mount the ring dressed in their *kesho-mawashi* (*facing page*). Note the basket of salt and water bucket.

As part of the dohyo-iri, rikishi raise their hands to show that they carry no weapons (*left*). The ring-entering ceremony of the yokozuna, or "grand champion," is a more complicated affair than that of the other rikishi (*below*). His elaborately knotted ceremonial belt can weigh over thirty pounds (*lower left*).

Sumo's all-purpose laborer, the *yobidashi* or "ring announcer," gets his moment in the spotlight as he announces the names of the next two competing rikishi from the center of the ring. To the left, the referee solemnly waits his turn to take control of the action.

Two rikishi perform *shiko*. This raising and stamping of the feet is intended as both a warming-up exercise and a symbolic exorcism of demons.

Salt-throwing is intended to purify the ring (*right*). Rikishi squat and try to stare each other down, part of the pre-bout psychological warfare that surrounds *shikiri*, or "toeing the mark" (*below*). The staring continues even after the two men stand and prepare to return to their corners for more salt (*below right*).

Rikishi lunge toward each other with surprising speed at the initial charge. *Tsuppari* or "slapping" is a technique favored by many rikishi as a means of keeping opponents off balance *(below left)*. An inside grip on the belt with the right hand will help the attacking rikishi drive his rival back and out of the ring *(below)*.

After being forced to the edge of the ring, the rikishi on the left is about to fall victim to a *nage* or "throwing" technique.

making up the circle are set slightly outside the others. In the days of outdoor sumo, this feature allowed rainwater to drain off.

A wooden roof of a design associated with Shinto shrines covers the ring. From its corners are hung four large tassels, signifying the cardinal directions and the seasons of the year: a green tassel symbolizing the east and spring; a red tassel for the south and summer; a white tassel for the west and autumn; and a black tassel representing the north and winter. The alignment of the directions, colors, and seasons reflects ancient Chinese cosmological theory. Until 1952, the roof over the dohyo was supported by four large poles wrapped in the appropriately colored cloth, but as these interfered with the view, especially after TV coverage began, they were removed. This roof is now suspended from the stadium roof by means of cables, and the symbolic meanings of the cloth-covered poles are now conveyed by the tassels.

The dohyo is sacred and is consecrated in a purification ceremony, the *dohyo-matsuri*, that takes place the day before each tournament begins. In this ceremony three white-garbed senior referees, who for sumo-associated rituals function as Shinto priests, invoke the blessings of the gods on the coming event. The ring is then consecrated by burying propitious offerings such as rice, seaweed, and dried fish in an earthenware pot in the center of the ring. An offering of salt and saké, their whiteness and clarity symbolizing purity, is then made. Once the ring has been purified, no one may stand on it except the rikishi themselves and others with business there; no one in shoes, of course, and absolutely no women.

Each day the ring is cleaned before and after the bouts, according to prescribed ritual. The spilling of blood during a bout is cause for great concern; if such a defilement should occur, the offending area is scraped clean, brushed, and inspected with much seriousness before the bouts are allowed to proceed. The rikishi themselves take great care to enter the ring in as clean and pure a state as possible. To this end you will see them wipe the sweat from their brows and underarms just before a bout begins. Even before mounting the dohyo, they rinse their mouths with water, using a ladle offered to them either by the winner of the previous bout, or, if their side has lost, its representative in the next bout. Once on the dohyo, the throwing of salt, again for purification, forms an important part of the pre-bout posturing, the subject of the next chapter. According to the Sumo Association, more than forty-five kilograms (one hundred pounds) of salt are flung into the ring each day.

CHAPTER 7

Psychological Warfare

A rikishi has three basic weapons. The first is physical; it consists of strength and speed developed through training. The second is technical and comprises the skills and techniques acquired through experience. The third, but by no means the least important, is psychological. Since a sumo bout really begins as a psychological confrontation, this latter merits some discussion. It is also, at least to Westerners, one of the more unusual aspects of the sport.

Before each bout, the names of the participants are called out by a *yobidashi*, or announcer. Dressed in kimono and traditional workman's leggings, he mounts the dohyo and slowly unfolds a white fan. Facing east and west in turn, he extends his fan and calls out the name of the rikishi representing each side in a quivering, theatrical voice. As previously mentioned, the east and west division no longer has any geographical basis but is maintained as an organizing device for tournament bouts and rankings. Matches are announced a day in advance throughout the tournament and cannot be changed. If a rikishi must drop out after the announcement, the bout counts as a loss for him and a win by default for his opponent.

The yobidashi descends from the dohyo as the two combatants mount it from their respective sides. As they begin their warming-up exercises, their names are announced once more, this time by the referee, called a *gyoji*, in a shout that begins powerfully but then fades in volume. If the bout is between top-division rikishi, other yobidashi, carrying pennants, may mount the dohyo and parade around it. The additional banners they carry represent prize money offered by sponsors to the winner of the bout; the pennants are advertisements for the sponsors, for example Tokyo Disneyland. Before a particularly crucial bout or a match between archrivals, a dozen or so sponsor pennants may appear, each worth about U.S. $600. Actually, only about half of the money from these goes directly to the winner; the rest goes into a fund set up to take care of the rikishi's taxes and retirement, and to the Sumo Association for "expenses."

Following an initial flexing of muscles and stamping of feet at the edge of the ring, the rivals go to opposite corners and rinse their mouths with a ladle of *chikara-mizu*, or "power water," provided by a fellow competitor. After wiping their lips with a piece of special white paper called *chikara-gami*, or "paper of strength," they pick up a handful of salt and heave it over the dohyo. Both of these gestures are acts of ritual purification that have been performed before bouts for more than three centuries.

Next, the rikishi squat near the center of the ring and face each other from a respectful distance. They fix each other with piercing stares, pound the dohyo, stand, slap themselves, and generally try to scare the hell out of each other. This ritual, known as *shikiri,* is often unimpressive to those whose definition of competition encompasses only its physical dimension. For most Western fans of TV sports, shikiri seems a good time for a commercial break. But for the true aficionado, this posturing is an intrinsic part of the spectacle, and veteran fans even claim to be able to pick a winner on the basis of a rikishi's performance during this ritual.

It might seem incredible that a 135-kilogram (three hundred-pound) professional competitor could ever be psyched out. But these rikishi fight each other often, and each is well aware of his opponent's relative skills, strengths, and weaknesses—even his fears and aspirations. To stare a rival straight in the eye takes concentration and will, and it is readily apparent if one is "off" physically or psychologically. Four minutes are allotted for the repetition of shikiri in the Makunouchi division, three for rikishi in Juryo. Those in the lower divisions have time for only a perfunctory glare or gesture.

During the sekitori's performance, the squatting, standing, staring, and salt throwing is repeated several times. The full allotted time does not have to be used; whenever the rikishi feel ready they can leap from the crouching position and clash in a coordinated move called the *tachi-ai,* or "initial charge."

If the two contenders continue shikiri for the full four minutes, a judge will eventually call time and indicate that the period of preparation is over. After wiping their faces and armpits, the rikishi crouch and face each other for the last time. The referee holds his fan flat against his forearm to signal that the bout must begin, but the rikishi themselves decide when to go. There is no precise signal for the start of the tachi-ai; the charge is naturally and spontaneously synchronized. Rikishi are huge men, but the speed of their forward lunge at this moment can be breathtaking and often results in a resounding "thwack" when their bodies or heads meet.

Some rikishi prefer to go directly for their opponent's *mawashi* or belt, as a good grip on the mawashi is considered a key to victory. Others, however, prefer to push and slap their opponents backward, keeping them continually off-balance, and still others may sidestep their opponent's initial charge. A wide range of offensive and defensive techniques are employed (the subject of Chapter 8), but the rules of sumo are simple and straightforward. The loser is the first rikishi to be forced out of the ring or to touch the ground with any part of his body other than the soles of his feet. There are also some proscribed tactics: striking with a closed fist, poking the eyes, pulling the hair, kicking the stomach, choking, bending an opponent's fingers back, and grabbing any part of the mawashi that covers the genital area.

It is the gyoji's responsibility to keep the action going. As soon as the tachi-ai commences, he begins to sidestep quickly around the rikishi, yelling out, *"Nokotta, nokotta!"* meaning, roughly, "You're still in there!" Occasionally, an extended period of grappling and shoving results in no advantage gained by either side, and the rikishi stand in the center of the ring locked in each other's grip. Although they appear drained and immobile, a close look shows an occasional flexing of the muscles as they test each other's capacity to resist a pull or shove. At such times the referee yells out, *"Yoi! Hakkeyoi!"* or "Keep it going!" On rare occasions the match is treated as a temporary stalemate and the rikishi retire to their respective sides to wipe down, rinse out their mouths and catch their breath. After this brief break they return to the center of the ring where the referee, with advice from the judges, directs them back into exactly the same position they were in before the match was halted. There are no ties in sumo; sooner or later, someone goes down or out.

The gyoji decides the winner or loser of a bout and no rikishi will question his decision, although ringside judges can and do, as will be seen in Chapter 10. When the winner of a bout has been decided, the vanquished party makes a curt bow to his opponent and retires. There is little show of emotion on the part of either winner or loser; to gloat or sulk is considered bad form. The gyoji raises his fan and announces the name of the victor. He then squats and presents the envelopes containing the cash prizes for the victory on the flat side of his fan. The winning rikishi makes three deft chops in the air with his hand, signifying thanks to the three Shinto deities of victory, and then picks up the envelopes. Before leaving the auditorium, he offers a ladle of water to the next competitor from his side.

In the old days of outdoor sumo, fans would signal their approval of a bout by throwing things into the ring for the winner, often money or kimono. That practice was eliminated as being unseemly, although after a really exciting match you may see appreciative fans seated in the box seats throw their cushions onto the dohyo. This mild display of exuberance is about as rowdy as the audience gets, which is surprising, considering the quantities of beer and saké consumed over the course of the day. Sumo fans are for the most part well-dressed and well-mannered, though they are enthusiastic and quite vocal. Favored rikishi are encouraged with shouts of "*Ganbatte!*" or "Go for it!", and those less well-liked may hear "*Makeru zo!*" or "You're going to lose!"

Following the last bout, a lower-ranked rikishi performs an interesting ceremony involving the twirling of a long bow. Called the *yumitori-shiki*, this ritual is said to date from the Edo period when the fourth yokozuna, Tanikaze, received a bow from the shogun upon defeating his archrival Onogawa. This display brings the tournament day officially to a close. But before leaving the stadium, the next chapter will examine more carefully some of the favored techniques used by the rikishi to win.

CHAPTER 8

Sumo Techniques

By the end of the preliminary posturing the rikishi has, or should have, made up his mind how he will handle the imminent onrush of his rival. As we mentioned in the previous chapter, some like to go straight for the mawashi, or belt, securing their preferred grip. Others invariably choose not to do so. They prefer to slap an opponent toward the edge of the ring using a technique called *tsuppari,* and then, when their man is off-balance, push him out. Both Akebono and Musashimaru excel at this type of sumo and are able to deliver thrusts to an opponent's upper chest, throat, and face sufficiently powerful enough to force him out, without ever needing to get ahold of his body or belt.

A victory by this method is called *tsukidashi,* or "thrust-out," if the loser is driven outside the ring, or *tsukitaoshi,* or "thrust-down," if he is knocked down. These techniques should not be confused with *oshidashi,* or "push-out."

There are seventy official winning techniques in sumo as recognized by the Japan Sumo Association. Illustrated here are some of the more common ones. The attacking rikishi is in the black *mawashi*.

Maki-otoshi

Uwatenage   Hatakikomi   Yorikiri   Tsukitaoshi

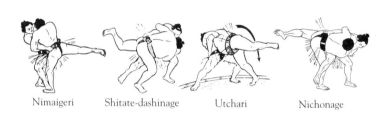

Nimaigeri   Shitate-dashinage   Utchari   Nichonage

Sotogake   Uchigake   Oshitaoshi   Kubinage

Uwate-dashinage   Watashikomi   Kotenage

Sukuinage   Kirikaeshi   Katasukashi   Tsuridashi

Hiki-otoshi   Ketaguri   Tottari   Abisetaoshi

Uchimuso   Shitatehineri   Okuridashi   Mitokoro-zeme

Uwatehineri   Kekaeshi   Shitatenage   Koshinage

Oshidashi   Tsuki-otoshi   Tsukidashi

Another of the most common winning techniques is the *oshitaoshi*, or "push-down." With oshidashi and oshitaoshi, continuous hand contact with the opponent is maintained.

Tsuppari is a valuable weapon in a rikishi's arsenal. Although a physically demanding tool, it can be used to set up almost any one of sumo's seventy winning techniques. If a rikishi senses that his opponent is overanxious to launch into his tachi-ai, he may simply sidestep the charge, turn, and slap his off-balanced opponent down with a swift and hard smack on the back. This technique, called *hatakikomi*, has caught many a fan napping and caused him or her to miss the bout. Kasugafuji and Kyokudozan both frequently employ this technique, although all rikishi use it at one time or another.

As exciting as a good burst of tsuppari is, there are many fans who prefer to watch the grappling techniques of sumo. With several noted exceptions, it is the heavier rikishi who naturally prefer to take the fullest advantage of their weight by coming to grips with their opponent as quickly as possible. In the clinch, the best advantage is obtained by having a grip on the opponent's mawashi with one hand inside his arm. If this is done with the left hand, it is called *hidari-yotsu*; if it is done with the right hand, it is called *migi-yotsu*. Having both hands on an opponent's belt inside his arms is a position called *morozashi*. A rikishi will try to keep an opponent from getting a grip by "flicking" his hips away from the gripping hand and by keeping the lower part of his body at a safe distance.

Taller men are usually more adept at these maneuvers, an advantage offset by their higher centers of gravity.

Once a grip on the mawashi is secured, a tactic favored by the bigger men is to use their weight advantage to gradually edge their opponents toward the edge of the dohyo and gently march them out. Known as *yorikiri*, this is also a very common winning technique. A more exciting variant is *yoritaoshi*, in which the vanquished, locked tightly in the grip of the victor, goes hurtling out of the ring and crashes to the ground.

Kirishima is one of several rikishi who have made a name for themselves using *tsuridashi*, or "lift-out." These rikishi like to grasp an opponent's mawashi firmly with both hands, push or pull him around until he is off-balance, and finally hoist him high in the air and out of the ring; against some rivals it is a truly Herculean feat. Then there's the spectacular *utchari*, or "backward pivot throw." This occurs when a rikishi, on the point of being toppled out, digs in at the edge of the ring, hoists his rival up over his stomach and, with a quick turn, flings him behind and out. This is a desperation technique that might be used by anyone, although the previously mentioned Kyokudozan is somewhat of an utchari specialist.

Other tactics are aimed at dumping a man inside the ring. Some rikishi are adept at using their legs to trip an opponent. One such technique is called *uchigake*, or "inside leg trip." Timing his move carefully, the attacker will suddenly thrust a leg through his rival's legs and upset him with a neat trip, wrapping his left leg around his opponent's right or his right around the opponent's left. Others favor *sotogake*, the "outside leg trip," in which a leg is wound outside the opponent's with the same result.

Uwatenage is an arm throw by which lighter men, such

as the legendary yokozuna Chiyonofuji, would often defeat much heavier opponents. It is translated as "overarm throw," the "over" referring to the hand that is outside the other man's arm. The throw is executed with this outside gripping hand. The opposite of this maneuver is *shitatenage*, or "underarm throw," using the power of the inside hand. Takanohana makes frequent use of this throw. More often than not a lot of maneuvering takes place, and several fruitless attempts are made at a variety of techniques before an opponent is finally caught off-balance and flung down.

Over the centuries, the number of winning techniques has varied as some technique designations became popular and others were discarded because they were considered minor variations of more common techniques. Today, professional sumo's governing body, the Japan Sumo Association, recognizes seventy winning techniques, or *kimarite*. To describe them all would require a volume in itself, but a study of the line drawings on pages 58–59 will allow fans to recognize those most commonly used.

A tournament is won by the top-division rikishi who has racked up the best win-loss record over the fifteen days of competition. The victory is called a *yusho*, and, if the rikishi's record is unblemished by even a single loss, it is referred to as a *zensho yusho*. In the old days, the yusho would go to the higher ranked man in case of tying records, but nowadays a playoff bout is held instead. If two rikishi finish on the last day with identical winning records, they will meet in an extra bout after the closing ceremony. On occasion, this has resulted in two top rikishi fighting twice in a row on the last day, quite an exciting windup for a tournament.

Each division of sumo has a tournament winner, but the focus is naturally on the winner of the top, Makunouchi, division. That lucky rikishi receives an incredible variety and quantity of prizes and trophies in a ceremony held after the last bout on the last day. Foremost among the spoils is the Emperor's Cup and a banner attesting to his victory given by the Sumo Association. He is also given a number of practical prizes from various national or local organizations and companies, including large quantities of dried mushrooms, whiskey, rice, and other goods.

As exciting as they are, tournaments are not necessarily the best place to watch rikishi in action. A much better, and often cheaper, seat can usually be obtained for one of the provincial exhibitions held in various locations several times a year during the off-season between tournaments. Called *jungyo*, or "rural tours," they are undertaken to promote sumo in areas where it is not normally seen. The regions are fixed but the schedule varies; it can be obtained by calling or writing in Japanese to the Japan Sumo Association just prior to the end of each tournament (the address and telephone number are listed on page 99).

CHAPTER 9

The Grand Champions

The title yokozuna, or "grand champion," as it is often translated, comes from the large white hawser (thick rope) these men wear around their waists as symbols of their rank. For the etymology fans out there, the term comes from the joining of two Japanese characters, *yoko*, meaning "side," and *tsuna*, meaning "a great rope." Although the actual origins of the yokozuna are lost in history, a popular theory stems from events that happened at a tournament in the early ninth century.

A wrestler from Omi province by the name of Hajikami was competing in a tournament held at a Shinto shrine. A regular powerhouse of a man, he was dropping the competition left, right, and center. Finally, the referee, looking to make the tournament a bit more interesting, grabbed the sacred rope that marked off the front of the shrine, wrapped it around Hajikami's waist and proclaimed that anyone who could lay a hand on the rope would be declared the victor. Legend has it that no one came close, and this is how the term yokozuna became associated with sumo's best.

Yokozuna was originally an honorary title conferred on only the very strongest ozeki, and the first written record of its use dates from 1773. Around that time it was a common practice to invite ozeki to perform at the groundbreaking ceremony of an important structure, such as a palace or villa. The Yoshida clan, a powerful family of among other things, sumo referees, decided to bestow a kind of license on the very best of the ozeki, proclaiming them yokozuna and certifying that these few men were the most qualified to participate in the groundbreaking events.

In spite of the general acceptance of this title, the highest rank on the banzuke, or official listing of rank, remained ozeki until 1890, when sumo's governing body decided to make yokozuna the pinnacle of the sumo world in fact as well as in name. One would think that such a change was the result of some major philosophical development on the part of sumo's council of elders. One would, in this case, be wrong. Actually, an impressive display of temper on the part of the sixteenth yokozuna, Nishinoumi I, more than anything else, created a need for the change.

A few years before the title yokozuna was added to the banzuke, it was decided that for each tournament the banzuke would hold only two ozeki within the thick border that frames it, one on the east side and one on the west. Any more than the chosen two would be placed *haridashi*, or "outside the border," a position that would be considered slightly lower in status. Heading into the May tournament that year, the powers-that-be found themselves with four ozeki. One of the four, Nishinoumi I, had just received his yokozuna certification from the Yoshida clan. He also had the worst record of the lot in the previous tournament, a fact that made him the low man on the totem pole.

When Nishinoumi I heard that he was going to wind up in a haridashi position, he went through the roof, telling the Association something to the effect of, "Where do you get off treating a newly appointed yokozuna so shabbily and who the heck do you think you are, anyway?" After much administrative soul-searching, the Association members decided that the best way to calm Nishinoumi while maintaining the integrity of the banzuke was to put his new title before his name, thus making it an official part of the rankings. Japanese society being heavily precedent-oriented, the practice stuck.

Akebono is the sixty-fourth yokozuna in this rank's three hundred-odd year history. Each individual who has held the rank has had his own colorful story, some filled with success, some tragedy. Any discussion of the yokozuna however, would be incomplete without a look at the achievements of four truly great men: Futabayama, Taiho, Kitanoumi, and Chiyonofuji. In modern times, these four did more than any other individuals to establish the tsuna as a symbol of sumo performed at the very highest level.

The first of this eminent group, Futabayama, was the thirty-fifth yokozuna and is considered by many to be one of sumo's gods. In spite of being blind in one eye and missing a right pinky due to two separate childhood accidents, he achieved a dominance of the sport that is still looked upon with awe. Not much to talk about in his early career, he blossomed when he made sumo's third-highest rank, sekiwake, in May 1936. He then proceeded to race up the ranks all the way to yokozuna without dropping a match. In the process, he set a still-unbroken record for consecutive top-division victories, at sixty-nine. He wound up his career in 1945, having won twelve top-division titles, eight of them with perfect records, all the while being just a little taller and a little lighter than the present Wakanohana.

The second on our list of legends is the forty-eighth yokozuna, Taiho. The dominant force in sumo through much of the Sixties, the half-Russian Taiho was a big man for his time, standing 1.87 meters (6 feet 1.5 inches) tall and weighing a solid 150 kilograms (331 pounds) in his prime. A handsome man, he was so popular with female fans that when he first entered the top division back in 1960, it was not uncommon for the women's side of public bath houses to mysteriously empty out when it was time for his matches to be shown on television. Many of the youth records that the present Takanohana has had so much fun breaking were once held by this Hokkaido native. One of his records that still stands, and the one that looks pretty safe for the foreseeable future, is the record he set for most top-division titles. Taiho embraced the Emperor's Cup a whopping thirty-two times!

The fifty-fifth yokozuna, Kitanoumi, was another giant of a man, standing 1.8 meters (5 feet 10 3/4 inches) and weighing 164 kilograms (364 pounds). In spite of his great bulk, he had one of the fastest tachiai, or initial charges, ever seen. His first claim to fame was the record he set as the youngest man ever promoted to yokozuna. He achieved sumo's highest rank after the 1974 Nagoya Tournament at the tender age of twenty-one years, two months. He went on to hold this rank with honor for ten years, finally retiring during the 1985 New Year's Tournament. During his reign at the top, he set records for the most consecutive top-division tournaments, winning ten bouts or more in thirty-seven tournaments, and most consecutive top-division tournaments making kachi-koshi, or winning a majority of matches, at fifty consecutive tournaments. He won the Emperor's Cup an impressive twenty-four times, third on the all-time list in this category.

The last of our quartet of legendary yokozuna will go down in history as the last of the great "little" yokozuna. Chiyonofuji, the fifty-eighth man to hold the rank, never weighed more than 120-odd kilograms (270 pounds) throughout his long and illustrious career—this in an age when the average top-division rikishi weighed a good eighteen to twenty-three kilograms (forty to fifty pounds) more. When he was promoted after only three tournaments as an ozeki back in July 1981, most experts felt that, at his size, he'd be lucky to survive more than two to three years and win six to eight top-division titles. By the time he retired in May 1991, he had set an impressive series of career achievement records, including most career wins at 1,045, and most Makunouchi division wins at 807. One of the achievements he will probably most be remembered for is a record he came tantalizingly close to breaking. Chiyo, in spite of his size and weight disadvantages, came two top-division titles away from breaking a record that many felt was unassailable. By the time he retired, he had won the Makunouchi division championship thirty-one times.

The promotion process for yokozuna centers around the Judges' Division and an advisory body to the Sumo Association called the Yokozuna Promotion Council. Formed in 1950, this group functions as a kind of watchdog commission for the rank, serving as the Association's access point to public opinion. The council is composed of a variety of individuals who have two things in common: they have all achieved a great degree of success in their chosen fields and they are all serious sumo fans.

The yokozuna selection process is a demanding one, for, unlike with lower-ranked rikishi, there is no danger of demotion for a yokozuna. If he fails to live up to the high standards of the rank, the only thing he can do is retire. The basic requirement for promotion is to win two consecutive tournaments ranked at ozeki, or to come up with two consecutive records that approximate a championship record, what those in the game call "runner-up honors." At the same time, the Council and the Association look at things such as character, deportment, and whether the individual in question can represent sumo with the kind of class the Japanese people expect.

Once the formal announcement of the promotion is made, the new yokozuna will become one very busy individual. His stablemates and sekitori from related stables will gather to make his new tsuna in a rather festive ceremony called a *tsuna-uchi*. After a fitting to make sure it sits right, the new yokozuna will rehearse his ring-entering ceremony under the watchful eye of one of his retired predecessors. After that, a special attestation ceremony is held at Tokyo's Meiji Shrine, one of Japan's most important religious centers. In this ceremony, the new tsuna is blessed and the yokozuna receives it, along with his certificate of promotion, from the chairman of the Japan Sumo Association. He then performs his ring-entering ceremony for the first time publicly in front of the shrine's main hall. The new yokozuna is now officially the living symbol of a sport and cultural activity that is thousands of years old. The honors and rewards are great, but so is the responsibility.

There are no set limits on the number of men allowed to hold the rank of yokozuna; there have been as few as none and as many as four at one time. The statisticians tell us that about one in seven hundred rikishi actually make this rank, and many a great ozeki have come as close as one win and failed to gain promotion. At the same time, many a strong ozeki have been promoted only to see his career shortened by the pressure that comes with standing at the pinnacle of sumo's hierarchy. And yet the eight hundred or so men competing in professional sumo at any one time all begin their careers with one dream in mind: the dream of being recognized as sumo's best, the dream of becoming a yokozuna.

CHAPTER 10

Referees and Judges

The gyoji, or referee, in sumo takes a role of far greater importance than does his counterpart in Western sports. He is, in fact, a leading player in the theater of sumo, without whom the show literally could not go on.

Some of the gyoji's varied and important duties were discussed in previous chapters. To summarize: he oversees the action in the ring, signals the start of the bouts, keeps the action going, and declares the winner and awards any prize money offered at the end of the match. He also has important ceremonial functions: he consecrates the ring and heads the retinue of the yokozuna during their dohyo-iri.

Of course, one man is not responsible for all these tasks. There are many referees, arrayed in a hierarchy similar to that of the rikishi. The rank of a referee can be roughly determined by his costume: the more sumptuous the apparel, the higher the rank. The gyoji's specific rank can be determined from the color of his trimmings: the tassel hanging from his fan, and the braid and rosettes at the collar and cuffs of his heavy silk kimono. Trimmings for the highest-ranked *tate-gyoji*, or "head referee," are purple, while those for the tate-gyoji ranked second are purple and white. Referees at the sanyaku level (the three ranks below yokozuna) wear bright red, while other Makunouchi-level gyoji are adorned with red and white. Referees at the Juryo level wear green and white tassels and trim, while those below Juryo wear either green or black.

Referees begin their training around the age of fifteen or sixteen. Quite often the new recruits are young men with a passion for the sport greater than their size. Unable to achieve the necessary height and weight to meet the basic entry requirements, they have decided to stay in sumo as a referee. Once in, they will take the name of either Shikimori or Kimura, the two families that dominated the occupation during the Edo period. Referees from the two families can be distinguished by the slightly different manner in which they grip the fan when announcing the rikishi for a bout: those who are from the Shikimori clan turn their thumb and fingers upward, while the Kimura style has their referees turning thumb and fingers downward.

Trainees begin refereeing the bouts of the lowest-ranked rikishi and gradually work their way through the referee hierarchy as their technique and judgment improve. Promotion, however, does not come quickly or automatically. Advancement depends upon seniority and, as the total number of positions is fixed, the pace can be excruciatingly slow.

The referee continually tries to keep a good position to view the action, but there are many tough calls (*above*). A black-robed judge, or *shinpan*, keeps a wary eye on the proceedings (*below*). It is plain to see he is a former rikishi.

Whenever there is a disputed call, the five ringside referees gather in a *mono-ii* or "judges' conference" in the middle of the ring.

The *dohyo* is sacred ground; the yobidashi work periodically to keep its surface clean and smooth.

Getting a two-handed inside grip on the opponent's belt, called *morozashi*, gives a rikishi commanding control *(left)*. His unfortunate rival is soon flipped up, over, and out of the ring *(below)*.

Legendary yokozuna Chiyonofuji *(below)* coaches his stable junior Hokutoumi in the finer points of the yokozuna ring-entering ceremony upon the latter's promotion to sumo's highest rank. Lending a careful eye to the proceedings is Konishiki.

Akebono, the first foreigner to achieve sumo's highest rank of yokozuna, receives the symbol of the top division championship, the Emperor's Cup.

The last bout of each tournament day is followed by a bow-twirling ceremony. The day's sumo has come to an end.

Moreover, promotion can be delayed through the acquisition of excessive demerits during the course of a tournament, the penalty for making an erroneous judgment of a bout's victor. Given the simplicity of the criteria for besting an opponent, forcing him down or out, it might seem that a bad call would be out of the question. But quite often the two rikishi hit the ground nearly simultaneously. It takes keen attention and skill to be properly positioned to catch the errant elbow or knee that may have brushed the sand first.

To ensure that a fair call is made each time, a panel of five judges watches every bout. Called *shinpan*, they are seated at the center of three sides of the dohyo, with two seated to the left and one on the right side. All are well-known retired rikishi and are easily recognizable due to their size and their formal black attire. Since they outnumber the gyoji and are better positioned to witness the crucial determining moment of the bout, judges will occasionally dispute the referee's decision about the winner. When this occurs, the judges climb up on the dohyo and hold a brief conference known as a *mono-ii* (literally "to talk about matters"). Three possible courses of action can result from such a conference: to affirm the gyoji's decision, to reverse the decision, or to hold a rematch. Called *tori-naoshi*, these rematches take place immediately and are always a big hit with the fans, who like nothing better than a close contest.

To help maintain their concentration, judges perform their duties in shifts, with seven shifts being rotated throughout the day. Judges also change their seating positions from shift to shift to gain the experience of viewing the action from different vantage points. During shift changes, the ring is carefully wetted down and swept, especially on top of and just outside the partially buried straw bales, so that the evidence of a hand or foot outside the ring will be clearly visible.

All of these measures are taken to ensure scrupulous fairness and accuracy in determining bout winners, but even with such precautions the system has not been infallible. Press photographs in the past have proven that even conferences of judges have resulted in erroneous decisions.

One particularly notorious incident occurred in March 1969. A referee's decision that the great yokozuna Taiho had just won his forty-sixth consecutive victory was reversed by the judges after a mono-ii. Film footage and photos developed later showed that the judges were in error and that Taiho had clearly won. However, the decision stood, and Taiho's streak was snapped at forty-five. The saddest part of this story is the fact that the Association was planning to introduce access to video replay for the judges from this tournament. Technical problems delayed the introduction by one tournament, costing Taiho his last shot at the record for consecutive top-division wins. Video coverage of tournaments is now monitored in a separate room by two additional judges, who can report their decisions to the dohyo via a small earphone worn by the head judge.

Judges have other duties away from the dohyo. The two most important of these are the *banzuke-hensei*, the preparation of the ranking list for each tournament, and the *torikumi-hensei*, the match-making for each day's schedule.

The first of these tasks is accomplished three days after the end of each tournament. The work must be attended to quickly because there are usually promotions, often requiring a rikishi to make some preparations. A new Juryo rikishi, for example, will need a silk mawashi and an embroidered kesho-mawashi for the next tournament. Newly appointed yokozuna are particularly busy, as they must have their tsuna prepared, master the dohyo-iri for their rank and be formally installed at Meiji Shrine.

The matching of rikishi for individual bouts is not fixed in advance, but takes place daily throughout the tournaments. This has been the cause of carping by some who feel that the pairings should be less manipulated, but the judges have a very sensible purpose in mind: to keep the tournament as exciting as possible. Those rikishi favored to take the yusho will usually not begin to meet each other until the beginning of the second week. By this time there may be three, four, or five rikishi with records good enough to still be in contention. If the judges are doing their job well and have a little luck going for them, the tournament winner will not emerge until the last day and then perhaps only after a thrilling, final, tie-breaking bout between two grand champions.

CHAPTER 11

What's in a Name?

A ring name, or *shikona*, is a symbol, and as with all symbols of sumo, it is accorded great respect and is never taken lightly. Selection of a proper shikona is vital. Yet as important as it is to the rikishi who bears it, he often has little choice in its selection. He may be allowed some opinion in the matter, but the stablemaster often makes the final choice based on stable tradition, custom, and his own expectations for the rikishi being named. A proper shikona links the rikishi to something powerful, and the association is a source of strength. The connection may be to an important natural feature sacred to Shinto, or perhaps to a past star who fought out of the same stable. A look at some of the names popular in the sumo world should help to make this clear.

Two of the most common characters found in rikishi names are *yama* and *fuji*. The former is the Japanese for "mountain," while the latter is usually written with the characters used in the name of Japan's Mount Fuji. A mountain, of course, is the perfect natural metaphor for a rikishi: broad at the base, majestic in stature, imperturbable, and immovable. A logical choice for a particular mountain would be Mount Fuji itself, Japan's tallest peak and a symbol of the nation that is also sacred to Shinto. Fuji forms part of the names of the rikishi Kasugafuji, Kotofuji, and Minatofuji, while yama appears in Musoyama and Wakanoyama, among others.

Not every rikishi can be a mountain, however. Some will turn to other symbols of strength, using names that include *kawa*, or *gawa* when it appears in combination, meaning "river," or *umi*, meaning "sea." One can see that an ocean is majestic and powerful, but a river is not so obviously awe-inspiring. In Eastern tradition, however, water is considered efficacious in many ways. Taoist texts use water as a symbol of virtuous power: it seeks the lowest level yet benefits all things, it moves slowly but ultimately overcomes anything in its path. And in Shinto, water is a purifying agent. Rikishi rinse their mouths with it before bouts, just as visitors do before entering the precincts of Shinto shrines. Although the use of "kawa" has become less popular of late, the character for "sea" can be found in the ring name of one of the most popular "little men" around, Mainoumi.

There are also several other names incorporating water-related words. The *izumi* in Mitoizumi means "spring," for example. The Japanese word for island, *shima*, forms part of the shikona of several rikishi, including Akinoshima and Kirishima. Like a mountain, an island is an enduring, immovable natural feature. It is a logical component of names of participants in the traditional sport of an island nation. Indeed, the Japanese are a patriotic—some would say nationalistic—people. It is therefore not surprising that *kuni* and *koku*, variant pronunciations of the character for "country," form part of some rikishi names. The name of the sixty-second yokozuna, Onokuni, means "Big Country," appropriate for the man who was a 202.5-kilogram (450-pound) behemoth, while that used by Kyokudozan's stablemaster when he was competing, Asahikuni, means "Land of the Rising Sun."

As they do in the West, the dragon and phoenix figure prominently in Oriental mythology. In the East, however, the dragon is not a fire-breathing kidnapper of damsels but a benevolent creature whose appearance heralds good fortune. Dragons are also closely associated with water in the East; they dwell in rivers and lakes and are credited with bringing life-sustaining rain. The Japanese for dragon is *ryu*, which forms part of the names of the tenth yokozuna, Unryu, or "Cloud Dragon," and a former sekitori active in the mid-1980s, Tamaryu (literally "Jewel Dragon"). A popular former sekiwake competing around the same time, Ho-o, had an interesting name made up of the characters for the male and female phoenix, a mythical bird said to appear only in times of peace and prosperity. The phoenix of the Orient is quite a splendid bird, supposedly 1.83 meters (six feet) in height with feathers of five colors, symbolizing the five cardinal virtues of Confucianism. The etymology of the characters for phoenix indicate that it is the emperor of birds and, like the Emperor of Japan, it is closely associated with the sun and with yang, the powerful, male principle of the universe.

Indeed, the symbol of Japan is the rising sun, which can be signified by a character pronounced *asahi*, which forms part of the name of the sixty-third yokozuna, Asahifuji (literally "Sunrise Over Mount Fuji"). The shikona of some rikishi incorporate the character for "brocade," read *nishiki*. This derives from the earlier days of sumo when bolts of embroidered silk were given as prizes to winning rikishi. Some active rikishi with this character in their names are Kotonishiki, or "Japanese Harp Brocade," and Konishiki, meaning "Little Brocade." The latter seems a rather dainty name for someone who weighs more than a quarter of a ton, but it was formerly used by a great rikishi from the same stable.

Characters taken from shikona of former sumo greats are often assigned to promising rikishi. For example, Chiyonoyama was an outstanding rikishi in the 1940s. His name means "Mountain of a Thousand Generations." He joined the Dewanoumi stable in 1942 at the age of sixteen and was promoted to yokozuna, the first from Japan's northern island of Hokkaido, in 1951. He retired eight years later after winning six yusho and compiling a top division record of 366 wins and 149 losses. He subsequently opened a stable under the name of Kokonoe, where he trained the fifty-second yokozuna, Kitanofuji, or "Northern Fuji." A decade later he recruited another promising young rikishi from Hokkaido. In honor of his mentors, the new rikishi was given the name Chiyonofuji, meaning "Eternal Fuji."

Quite often, a rikishi's stable is evident from his name. If a rikishi's shikona starts with the previously mentioned asahi, or the variant reading *kyoku*, odds are he is fighting out of the Oshima stable, owned and managed by a former ozeki who fought under the ring name Asahikuni. There is also a proprietary approach to shikona. Any rikishi whose name begins with Dewa will belong to Dewanoumi Beya, and any whose name begins with Tatsu will hail from the Tatsunami Beya. In some cases, almost every rikishi in a stable will be given a name associated with it. The shikona of most of the members of Sadogatake Beya, for example, begin with Koto.

A rikishi may bear several names over the course of his association with sumo. He may change it in an attempt to improve his luck or to mark some particularly momentous event in his career. The sixty-first yokozuna, Hokutoumi, for example, formerly fought under his real name, Hoshi. He took the ring name Fujiwaka very early in his career but, after having a losing record in that first tournament with the new name, immediately went back to his family name. When he was promoted to ozeki, he assumed the ring name which means "Northern Victorious Sea," reflecting his Hokkaido origins.

Upon retirement, most top rikishi want to become members of the Japan Sumo Association. This entails the assumption of yet another name, since association members are limited to a fixed number of traditional surnames. Thus, Hokutoumi, not long after finishing his career in May 1992, took a fourth name, Hakkaku, which he will use until his mandatory retirement from the Association at the age of sixty-five.

Incidentally, in case you should be introduced to a top-ranked rikishi, which is not entirely unlikely if you are out on the town in the Ryogoku area, they are addressed with the honorific suffix *-zeki*, as in, for example, Musoyama-zeki. This derives from the term *sekitori*, used to denote men fighting in the top two divisions. Actually, rikishi are generally a friendly and well-behaved crowd and do not object to being addressed with *-san*, the ordinary Japanese suffix for surnames, but this is more often used with the names of lower-ranked rikishi.

CHAPTER 12

The Spoils of Victory

As with all other privileges and responsibilities in the world of sumo, monetary compensation is accorded by rank and differs widely between the top and bottom rungs of the sport. Only rikishi in the top two divisions, Juryo and Makunouchi, receive regular salaries. Yokozuna now earn $19,870 per month, ozeki $16,630, and so on down the line (dollar figures calculated at the rate of ¥100 to the dollar). Rikishi in the lower divisions must be content with an allowance for participation in each tournament, called a *basho teate*, ranging from approximately $900 for Makushita rikishi down to about $650 for rikishi in the Jonokuchi division. However, salaries alone do not give an accurate picture of the rewards of a career in sumo once a rikishi makes it to the top.

There are literally dozens of other forms of direct and indirect compensation for the higher ranking rikishi, such as supplementary allowances for Tokyo tournaments and travel allowances for provincial tours. There are a variety of special subsidies—one for the regular replacement of a yokozuna's tsuna, for example. There is also a separate form of compensation calculated on the basis of past performance. New rikishi are credited with a small amount, ¥3, when their name first appears on the banzuke, or official listing of rank. A half yen is added for each victory over kachi-koshi, or a simple majority of wins. When a rikishi attains sekitori status, he receives at each tournament the total he has accumulated multiplied by 2,500, on top of his basic salary. There are also bonuses added to this figure: ¥10 for a *kinboshi*, a victory over a yokozuna while holding a maegashira rank, ¥30 for a top-division title, and ¥50 if the title is won with a perfect 15-0 record. When it's all added up and multiplied by that 2,500, the final figure can be impressive. At the end of his career, the fifty-eighth yokozuna, Chiyonofuji, was receiving a total of over $36,000 in bonus money every tournament just for being listed on the banzuke as a sekitori.

There are also a variety of cash prizes: prizes for tournament victories in each class *(yusho)*; prizes for bout victories in the Makunouchi division *(kensho)*; and Makunouchi special prizes that come with awards for the display of "fighting spirit" (the *Kanto-sho*), technique (the *Gino-sho*), and for defeating the most ozeki and yokozuna (the *Shukun-sho*). Then there are gifts from supporters and fan clubs, honorariums for participation in public and private events and, when a top-division rikishi's fighting days are over, a large retirement bonus from the Japan Sumo Association. In fact, the total earnings by a successful rikishi over a lifetime can be enormous and are virtually impossible for anyone but a trained accountant with a minor in detective work to calculate with any degree of accuracy.

But it can be fun to try. Take, for example, the case of one of the greatest yokozuna in modern sumo history, Chiyonofuji (now Kokonoe Oyakata). Near the end of his career, he was receiving a monthly base salary of approximately $11,520. In addition to that, he received a $1,992 cumulative bonus for each tournament that his name appeared on the banzuke as a yokozuna. He was also getting over $50,000 from the Association for each tournament championship—he won thirty-one in his career—and between $3,000 and $4,500 in kensho for every match he won. Honorariums would range from $9,600 for an appearance at an autograph session to $28,800 for performing his dohyo-iri, or ring entering ceremony, at a Shinto shrine.

Chiyonofuji's popularity is reflected in the sizable gifts he received from supporters. After his victory in the 1988 Kyushu Basho, he was reportedly given $160,000 by his ecstatic fans. By late 1988, three years before his retirement, the weekly magazine *Shukan Shincho* estimated that Chiyonofuji had received around $6.4 million since attaining the rank of yokozuna. And when he finally retired from the sport, he received from the Sumo Association $1 million as a special bonus for his long years of service, along with the $400,000 he was due as his retirement bonus. He also kept a large percentage of the proceeds from his retirement ceremony, which is often an important part of a departing rikishi's retirement benefits. In his case, the sum had to be substantial because his ceremony wound up being one of the biggest in sumo history. The rewards for those who make it to the very pinnacle of this sport are truly great.

And what of life after sumo? As can be readily inferred, the career of the rikishi is not an easy one. To be battered and smashed by opponents weighing up to—and sometimes over—two hundred kilograms (440 pounds) for ninety days of regular tournament action a year, not to mention the countless practice and exhibition bouts, really takes its toll. The remarkable career of Chiyonofuji aside, most rikishi begin contemplating retirement as they near their thirties.

To mark the occasion of a rikishi's retirement, a special ceremony is held, called a *danpatsu-shiki*, which involves the ritual removal of his topknot. If the rikishi has met the proper criteria, he will have his retirement ceremony at the Kokugikan. Lower-rankers usually have theirs at the stable or a hotel. During the ceremony, the rikishi sits in a chair in the center of a dohyo, while his patrons, who have made a sizable donation for the privilege of participating, file forward one by one and snip off a few hairs, avoiding the topknot. The snipping is done with gold-plated scissors, held by a referee. The patrons are followed by fellow rikishi. Finally, the stablemaster himself steps forward and cuts off the topknot, which the rikishi may keep as a memento of his career in the sport.

A top-ranking rikishi usually stays in sumo after retirement by becoming an elder in the Japan Sumo Association, a prestigious position that guarantees an income until the mandatory retirement age of sixty-five. As the number of elders is fixed at 105, however, this option is obviously not open to every rikishi. Those aspiring to membership in this elite group must purchase a coach's name at considerable cost from a retiring elder. However, even with the mandatory retirement age, there is no guarantee that a name will be available when a rikishi retires. Many, therefore, make arrangements for acquiring a name long before they end their careers.

Exceptions are occasionally made to the rigid elder system. One rule allows yokozuna to become temporary elders for five years, during which time they can try to acquire the necessary name needed to make their status permanent. Two outstanding yokozuna of the modern era, Taiho and Kitanoumi, were both accorded the status of single-generation elder. This means they are allowed to keep their ring names for the length of their careers as coaches, but the positions will be abolished upon their retirements. The same status was granted to Chiyonofuji, but he decided to refuse the honor because of his desire to take over the Kokonoe stable. Only an elder in the Sumo Association is allowed to run a stable. Thus, there could theoretically be 105 stables, although, as we have seen, there are less than half that number. One of the newest is Hatachiyama beya, opened in June 1994 by the former ozeki Hokutenyu.

Traditionally, the higher up in rank a rikishi went, the shorter his life span. Since only fairly successful, i.e. highly ranked, men could afford to stay in the Association, coaches would often die before they reached retirement. Today, with better post-retirement health care, many coaches are living to retirement and well beyond, leading to an ever-increasing sparsity of unused, available names.

The most serious health problems faced by retired rikishi

are diabetes and heart trouble, due to their years of packing away chanko-nabe, rice, saké, and beer. They also typically have problems with tendons, ligaments, and joints. For these reasons, most rikishi begin to shed weight as soon as they retire. But they don't necessarily give up the chanko-nabe. Many of the rikishi who are unable to remain in the Association go into the restaurant business and specialize in serving the dish that they have been preparing and eating all their lives.

CHAPTER 13

The Lure of Sumo

What is the fascination of this sport of emperors? To the Japanese, this question is as strange as much of traditional oriental culture first appears to be to the average Westerner. Sumo is about as Japanese as one can get. Pajama-clad children grew up grappling, sumo style, on top of their bedding before an irate parent would tell them, for the last time, to go to bed. Up until not that long ago, every schoolyard in the country had a dohyo tucked away in one corner, and until the end of the Second World War sumo was a part of the Japanese physical education curriculum.

Japan is a country culturally in flux. The radical nature of the changes the Japanese are seeing today in daily life can be compared in many ways to the kind of cultural revolution that occurred during Japan's Meiji Restoration, that period in which a feudal state was dragged, often kicking and screaming, into the twentieth century. This time, though, the pressure is not coming from without but from within. The Japanese themselves are searching for a new meaning to the concept of "Japaneseness," what it means to be a Japanese, as they approach the twenty-first century. Many of the changes that have and are taking place have forced much of what is considered traditional Japanese culture to the brink of extinction.

And yet sumo survives. It has had its ups and downs in popularity and will continue to do so, but it survives. In fact, it has more than survived; it has flourished. Today it is more popular than ever, and although the Japanese may take a somewhat different approach to it than they have in the past, it is still as much a part of Japanese society as it ever was.

What does this mean to the foreign fan? For starters, it means that sumo is one of the best doorways into the traditionally closed society that is Japan. It offers a way to understand Japanese thinking that is unique in its accessibility and ease of comprehension. Anyone can watch sumo and, with a little effort, anyone can understand it. The structures that compose sumo society can be seen, in more diluted forms of course, in Japanese society at large.

A discussion of sumo's sociological significance is important in considering its popularity and its fascination, but two more important points should not be overlooked: that sumo is great sport and sumo is great theater. Sumo strikes a chord in both man's competitive and dramatic natures.

Man is a competitive beast, probably the most competitive around. We compete in everything we do and yet we can't get enough of competition in our daily lives, so we invent sport as a form of entertainment. In spite of our love of team sports and the cooperative philosophy they emphasize, we always break down team effort into an examination of individual achievement. In our minds, nothing is more intriguing than the individual rising to a challenge to achieve greatness. When this challenge involves going against an equally skilled opponent, the fascination can take on almost mythic proportions. Look at the millions of words devoted to discussions of the world's great boxers. Some of the best sports writing in the English-speaking world has been devoted to the intricacies and subtleties of these men, their great fights, and the world they have created for themselves.

Sumo is one-on-one competition in its purest form. There are no pads, masks, shin guards, helmets, gloves, or body armor. The competitors are almost naked: man at his most elemental. Yet the two men throw themselves at each other with a force that is as great as any contact sport the West has ever invented. I'm reminded of the first time someone came up with the idea of attaching microphones to NFL linemen so we could get a real feel for what it sounded like when those boys went to work. Awesome sounds they were, but they cannot compare to the sounds the NHK television mike mounted over the dohyo picks up every tournament day, when two 157-kilogram (350-pound) top-division behemoths crash into each other at full speed in the center of the ring.

As complex as the technique of the sport is, the rules are equally simple. Yet when you pursue a study of the sport with a fan's enthusiasm, you wind up discovering ever-deepening layers of complexity as your knowledge of the sport increases. As sport it offers everything a fan could want in terms of skill, depth, purity, and excitement. Yet sumo's fascination does not end there because, as we've discovered in the course of this book, sumo is a lot more than just another sport.

What makes it even more fascinating is the depth of the culture and tradition that permeates it. There is a pageantry and richness of color to sumo that is unlike any other athletic endeavor in the world. Like it's sportive aspects, the cultural and traditional aspects are piled one on top of the other in layer upon layer of nuance, meaning, and history. And as with those sportive aspects, as each layer is understood the appreciation of sumo increases. The various ring-entering ceremonies, the ceremonial aprons, the silk mawashi, the referees' costumes, tassels, salt, sweat, and sand—all these combine to form a glorious kaleidoscope of color and sound.

And then there is the atmosphere of the actual tournaments themselves. Historically, there have been very few places where the Japanese could loosen the old kimono (like the necktie today) and really enjoy themselves with abandon. Sumo has always offered one of those few venues available to the Japanese, and there is a kind of relaxed, infectious, fun atmosphere to a grand sumo tournament that is special. As a matter of fact, during that first period of dramatic postwar economic growth in this nation (when the Japanese were earning the dubious title of "economic animals"), tickets to sumo tournaments were considered one of the few acceptable excuses for leaving work early!

Sumo has action, drama, tradition, color, and a depth that reflects a history closely tied to the Japanese nation itself. What's the fascination? Perhaps a better question might be, once you get a taste of the sport, "How can one *not* fall in love with sumo?"

Chanko-nabe Restaurants

When in Tokyo, a real dining treat is a visit to one of the several restaurants that specialize in chanko-nabe, that one-pot sumo staple on every stable's menu. Although the Japanese prefer to eat this dish in winter, it is designed to be eaten all year long. Filled with meat, chicken, or fish and an assortment of vegetables, it is as nutritious as it is delicious. The sampling of restaurants listed below is guaranteed to add a new dimension to your sumo experience. And don't forget to call ahead, in Japanese, for reservations.

ICHINOTANI
2–10–2 Soto Kanda
Chiyoda-ku, Tokyo 101
Tel. (03) 3251–8500

HAMARIKI
2–14–5 Takadanobaba

Shinjuku-ku, Tokyo 169
Tel. (03) 3200–2901

KAWASAKI
2–13–1 Ryogoku
Sumida-ku, Tokyo 130
Tel. (03) 3631–2529

NARUYAMA
3–9–2 Kudan Minami
Chiyoda-ku, Tokyo 102
Tel. (03) 3261–1632

DAIKIRIN
1–1–11 Nezu
Bunkyo-ku, Tokyo 113
Tel. (03) 3823–5998

KIYOKUNI
2–14–23 Koishikawa
Bunkyo-ku, Tokyo 112
Tel. (03) 3816–5544

KITASEUMI
1–21–22 Nishi Koiwa
Edogawa-ku, Tokyo 133
Tel. (03) 3672–7393

TOMOEGATA
2–17–6 Ryogoku

Sumida-ku, Tokyo 130
Tel. (03) 3632–5600

TAMAKATSU
3–2–12 Negishi
Taito-ku, Tokyo 110
Tel. (03) 3872–8712

YOSHIBA
4–8–11 Ginza
Chuo-ku, Tokyo 104
Tel. (03) 3567–4481

IZUTSU
4–18–8 Shimbashi
Minato-ku, Tokyo 105
Tel. (03) 3434-5557

FURIWAKE
3–35–13 Yushima
Bunkyo-ku, Tokyo 113
Tel. (03) 3836–5888

Sumo Stable Addresses and Phone Numbers

Spectators are almost always welcome to watch morning practice at the stables, but it's always a good idea to call ahead first (the Futagoyama stable, due to the popularity of its top-ranked rikishi, does not welcome observers). The best thing to do when looking for permission to stop by the larger stables is to ask for the stable manager—not to be confused with the stablemaster—and to be sure you are ready to make all of your inquires in Japanese.

Foreigners are also often welcome to become members of rikishi or stable *koen-kai* (support groups). Here as well, the stable manager would be the man to steer you in the right direction.

AJIGAWA
1–7–4 Mori
Koto-ku, Tokyo 135
Tel. (03) 3634–5514

ARAKI
9562–2 Yaho
Kunitachi-shi, Tokyo 186
Tel. (0425) 76–4317

ASAHIYAMA
4–14–21 Kita Kasai
Edogawa-ku, Tokyo 134
Tel. (03) 3686–4950

AZUMAZEKI
4–6–4 Higashi Komagata
Sumida-ku, Tokyo 130
Tel. (03) 3625–0033

DEWANOUMI
2–3–15 Ryogoku
Sumida-ku, Tokyo 130
Tel. (03) 3632–4920

FUTAGOYAMA
3–10–6 Honcho
Nakano-ku, Tokyo 164
Tel. (03) 3375–2432

HAKKAKU
1–16–1 Kamezawa
Sumida-ku, Tokyo 130
Tel. (03) 3621–0404

HANAKAGO
3956–1 Uenohara
Uenohara-cho, Kita Tsuru-
    gun
Yamanashi-ken 409–01
Tel. (0554) 63–5578

HANAREGOMA
3–12–7 Minami Asagaya

Suginami-ku, Tokyo 166
Tel. (03) 3391–9748

IRUMAGAWA
3–32–12 Hachioji
Yono-shi, Saitama-ken
    338
Tel. (048) 858–5043

ISEGAHAMA
225–9 Matsugazaki
Kashiwa-shi, Chiba-ken
    227
Tel. (0471) 34–2535

ISENOUMI
3–17–6 Harue-cho
Edogawa-ku, Tokyo 132
Tel. (03) 3677–6860

IZUTSU
2–2–7 Ryogoku
Sumida-ku, Tokyo 130
Tel. (03) 3634–9827

KABUTOYAMA
5–19–7 Hongo
Bunkyo-ku, Tokyo 113
Tel. (03) 3811–9080

KAGAMIYAMA
8–16–1 Kita Koiwa
Edogawa-ku, Tokyo 133
Tel. (03) 3673–7339

KASUGANO
1–7–11 Ryogoku
Sumida-ku, Tokyo 130
Tel. (03) 3634–9828

KATAONAMI
1–33–9 Ishihara
Sumida-ku, Tokyo 130
Tel. (03) 3623–9596

KISE
2–35–21 Hongo
Bunkyo-ku, Tokyo 113
Tel. (03) 3811–6365

KITANOUMI
2–10–11 Kiyosumi
Koto-ku, Tokyo 135
Tel. (03) 3630–9900

KOKONOE
4–22–4 Ishihara
Sumida-ku, Tokyo 130
Tel. (03) 5608–0404

KUMAGATANI
1–6–28 Minami Koiwa
Edogawa-ku, Tokyo 133
Tel. (03) 3671–9511

MAGAKI
3–8–1 Kamezawa
Sumida-ku, Tokyo 130
Tel. (03) 3623–7449

MATSUGANE
4–13–1 Kosaku
Funabashi-shi, Chiba-ken
  273
Tel. (0473) 38–3081

MICHINOKU
971 Nagasaku-cho
Hanamigawa-ku,
Chiba-shi, Chiba-ken
  262
Tel. (043) 286–1951

MIHOGASEKI
3–2–12 Chitose
Sumida-ku, Tokyo 130
Tel. (03) 3632–4767

MINATO
2–20–10 Shibanakada
Kawaguchi-shi, Saitama-
  ken 333
Tel. (048) 266–0015

MINEZAKI
2–20–3 Tagara
Nerima-ku, Tokyo 179
Tel. (03) 5997–3601

MIYAGINO
4–6–13 Midori
Sumida-ku, Tokyo 130
Tel. (03) 3634–6291

MUSASHIGAWA
4–27–1 Higashi Nippori
Arakawa-ku, Tokyo 116
Tel. (03) 3802–6333

NAKAMURA
4–1–10 Chuo
Edogawa-ku, Tokyo 132
Tel. (03) 3655–1808

NARUTO
183 Hachigasaki
Matsudo-shi, Chiba-ken
270
Tel. (0473) 46–4110

NISHONOSEKI
4–17–1 Ryogoku
Sumida-ku, Tokyo 130
Tel. (03) 3631–0179

OGURUMA
2–15–5 Kiyosumi
Koto-ku, Tokyo 135
Tel. (03) 5245–5103

OSHIMA
3–5–3 Ryogoku
Sumida-ku, Tokyo 130
Tel. (03) 3631–9708

OSHIOGAWA
2–17–7 Kiba
Koto-ku, Tokyo 135

Tel. (03) 3643–9797

SADAGOTAKE
39 Minamimachi, Kushizaki
Matsudo-shi, Chiba-ken
271
Tel. (0473) 84–4973

SHIKIHIDE
4–17–17 Sanuki
Ryugasaki-shi, Ibaraki-ken
301
Tel. (0297) 66–9835

TAIHO
2–8–3 Kiyosumi
Koto-ku, Tokyo 135
Tel. (03) 3820–8340

TAKADAGAWA
2–1–15 Ichinoe
Edogawa-ku, Tokyo 132
Tel. (03) 3656–5604

TAKASAGO
1–16–5 Hashiba
Taito-ku, Tokyo 111
Tel. (03) 3876–7770

TAKASHIMA
3–21–2 Kami Isshiku
Edogawa-ku, Tokyo
133
Tel. (03) 5607–5488

TAMANOI
4–12–14 Umeda
Adachi-ku, Tokyo 123
Tel. (03) 3852–4333

TATSUNAMI
3–26–2 Ryogoku
Sumida-ku, Tokyo 130
Tel. (03) 3631–2424

TATSUTAGAWA
3–28–21 Shin Koiwa
Katsushika-ku, Tokyo 124
Tel. (03) 5662–0128

TOKITSUKAZE
3–15–3 Ryogoku
Sumida-ku, Tokyo 130
Tel. (03) 3634–8549

TOMOZUNA
1–20–7 Mori
Koto-ku, Tokyo 135
Tel. (03) 3631–6390

WAKAMATSU
3–5–4 Honjo
Sumida-ku, Tokyo 130
Tel. (03) 5608–3223

For anything else you need to know about sumo, you can always contact, in Japanese of course, the Sumo Association itself.

The Japan Sumo Association
1–3–28 Yokoami
Sumida-ku, Tokyo 130
Tel. (03) 3623–5111

Glossary of Sumo Terms

akeni   lacquered wickerware trunk used by rikishi in the top two divisions to carry their sumo gear

banzuke   the official listing of rank, revised and published before every tournament

basho   professional sumo tournament

basho-teate   an allowance given to rikishi for appearing in a tournament

bintsuke abura   scented hair pomade used to dress a rikishi's topknot

butsukari geiko   type of training in which one rikishi repeatedly tries to push his opponent out of the ring while that opponent braces himself to prevent it

chanko-nabe   a high-protein stew that is standard fare in a sumo stable

chikara-gami   paper of strength; used by rikishi in the top two divisions to wipe their mouths after receiving "water of strength"; serves as part of the pre-bout purification process

chikara-mizu   water of strength; used by rikishi in the top two divisions to rinse their mouths prior to bouts; serves as part of the pre-bout purification process

chonmage　rikishi hairstyle consisting of a simple topknot

danpatsu-shiki　topknot-cutting ceremony marking a rikishi's retirement

de-geiko　practice at a stable other than one's own

dohyo　the ring

dohyo-iri　ring-entering ceremony

dohyo matsuri　pre-tournament ceremony designed to purify the ring

Gino-sho　Technique Prize; top division special prize awarded to a rikishi ranked below ozeki who demonstrates outstanding technique over the course of a tournament

gohei　white, zigzag paper strips that hang from the front of a yokozuna's hawser

hatakikomi　slap down; one of the seventy winning techniques in sumo

heya　stable; where rikishi live and train

hidari-yotsu　left-hand inside grip; one of the basic gripping techniques in sumo in which the rikishi grabs his opponent's mawashi with the left hand inside the opponent's right

ichomage/o-icho　gingko leaf-shaped hairstyle that sekitori wear for tournaments and other formal occasions

Jonidan　second lowest of the six divisions in professional sumo

Jonokuchi　the lowest of the six divisions in professional sumo

jungyo　rural exhibition tours held after certain tournaments that take sumo to areas not often exposed to live performances

Juryo　the second highest of the six divisions in professional sumo; one of sumo's two privileged divisions

kachi-koshi　a winning tournament in which the rikishi wins more bouts than he loses; almost always a guarantee of promotion

Kanto-sho　Fighting Spirit Prize; the top-division special prize awarded to a rikishi ranked below ozeki who demonstrates the most fighting spirit over the course of a tournament *keiko*   general term for training or practice

kensho   a special cash prize awarded to the winner in certain top-division matches

kesho-mawashi   elaborately embroidered apron worn during the ring-entering ceremony performed by rikishi in the top two divisions

kimarite   general term for the winning techniques of sumo

kinboshi   a "gold star" awarded to any maegashira-ranked rikishi in the top division who defeats a yokozuna; worth an extra ¥25,000 bonus per tournament for the duration of the rikishi's career in the top two divisions

koen-kai   supporters' group or fan club for a rikishi ranked in the top two divisions or for a stable

Kokugikan   Japan's main sumo arena, located in Tokyo and home of three of the six tournaments held annually

komusubi   junior champion second grade; the fourth-highest rank in professional sumo

kotenage   armlock throw; one of the seventy winning techniques in sumo

kubinage   headlock throw; one of the seventy winning techniques in sumo

Kyokai   short for the Nihon Sumo Kyokai, or "Japan Sumo Association," the governing body of professional sumo

mae-zumo   a test competition for new recruits before their names appear on the official listing of rank

maegashira   the lowest ranking in the top division of professional sumo

make-koshi   a tournament performance resulting in a majority of losses

Makunouchi   the highest of the six divisions in professional sumo; one of sumo's two privileged divisions

Makushita   the third-highest division in professional sumo; the division immediately below Juryo

matawari   seated split stretch with the chest pressed to the ground

mawashi   a canvas or silk belt-like garment worn by rikishi .

migi-yotsu   a right-hand inside grip; one of the basic gripping techniques in sumo in which the rikishi grabs his opponent's mawashi with the right hand inside the opponent's left

mono-ii   conference of judges following a disputed bout

morozashi   a two-handed inside grip in which both hands grasp the mawashi inside the opponent's hands

moshiai-geiko   practice in which the winner takes on all challengers until he loses

oshi-dashi   frontal push-out; one of the most common pushing techniques and one of the seventy winning techniques in sumo

oshi-taoshi   frontal push-down; a variation on the above and one of the seventy winning techniques in sumo

oyakata   translated as either "coach" or "stablemaster"; this title is used after the names of the 107 elders of the Japan Sumo Association

ozeki   champion; the second highest rank in sumo

rikishi   gentleman of strength; the term used to describe professional sumo wrestlers

sagari   the cords attached to the front of the mawashi, made of cotton (for the lower ranks) or starched silk (for the top two divisions); worn when a rikishi competes

sanban-geiko   practice in which two rikishi fight a series of consecutive bouts

Sandanme   third lowest of the six divisions in professional sumo

sanyaku   the three top ranks below yokozuna

sekitori   rikishi ranked in one of the top two privileged divisions

sekiwake   junior champion; the third highest rank in sumo

shikiri   toeing the mark; the squatting from a variation of a four-point stance that precedes a sumo bout

shiko   a training exercise in which a leg is lifted parallel to the body as high as possible then driven downward in a stamping motion

shikona   ring name

shinpan   judge

shiranui   one of two styles of yokozuna ring-entering ceremony

shitatenage   underarm throw; a common "belt" technique and one of the seventy winning techniques in sumo

Shukun-sho   Outstanding Performance Award; the top-division special prize awarded to a rikishi ranked below ozeki who defeats the most yokozuna or ozeki over the course of a tournament

soto-gake   outer leg trip; one of the more common leg techniques and one of the seventy winning techniques in sumo

sumotori   a popular, if less accurate, term (than rikishi) used to describe professional sumo wrestlers

tachi-ai   initial charge

tachimochi   sword bearer; the rikishi who carries the yokozuna's sword during his ring-entering ceremony

tate-gyoji   the two highest-ranked referees in professional sumo

tawara   straw bales sunk into the dirt of the ring to form an inner circle and an outer square

tegata   a rikishi's autographed palm print; usually printed in red or black, these are popular souvenirs among supporters and fans

teppo   a training exercise involving the rhythmic slapping of a wooden pole with open hands

tokoyama   professional sumo hairdresser

torinaoshi   a rematch following a disputed bout

tsukebito   manservant; junior rikishi appointed to attend to rikishi in the top two divisions, coaches, and the top two referees

tsukidashi   thrust-out; one of the most common thrusting techniques and one of the seventy winning techniques in sumo

tsukitaoshi   thrust-down; a variation on the above and one of the seventy winning techniques in sumo

tsuna   white ceremonial hawser worn by the yokozuna; the symbol of the yokozuna rank

tsuppari   slapping or thrusting with open hands

tsuridashi   lift-out; one of the seventy winning techniques in sumo

tsuriotoshi   body drop throw; a variation on the above and one of the seventy winning techniques in sumo

tsuyu-harai   dew sweeper; the rikishi who serves as an usher for the yokozuna during his ring-entering ceremony

uchigake   inner leg trip; one of the seventy winning techniques in sumo

unryu   one of the two styles of yokozuna ring-entering ceremony *utchari*   backward pivot throw; one of the seventy winning techniques in sumo

uwatenage   overarm throw; a common "belt" technique and one of the seventy winning techniques in sumo

yobidashi   ring announcer; also serves as professional sumo's all-purpose laborer

yokozuna   grand champion; the top rank in sumo

yorikiri   frontal force-out; the most common "belt" technique and one of the seventy winning techniques in sumo

yoritaoshi   frontal force-down; a variation on the above and one of the seventy winning techniques in professional sumo

yumitori shiki   the bow-twirling ceremony that marks the conclusion of a tournament day

yusho   tournament championship

zensho yusho   a perfect tournament championship; a tournament victory with no losses

Other Titles in the
Tuttle Library of Martial Arts

AIKIDO AND THE DYNAMIC SPHERE
by Adele Westbrook and Oscar Ratti

> Aikido is a Japanese method of self-defense that can be used against any form of attack and that is also a way of harmonizing all of one's vital powers into an integrated, energy-filled whole.

BEGINNING T'AI CHI *by Tri Thong Dang*

> T'ai chi is a holistic method of self-healing, moving meditation, and a philosophical way of life. This handy guide introduces the "Simplified Tai Chi" form, which was specifically developed for beginners by China's Ministry of Physical Culture and Sports.

BEYOND THE KNOWN: THE ULTIMATE GOAL OF THE MARTIAL ARTS *by Tri Thong Dang*

> A novel that illustrates one man's quest to find the way of the martial arts. A work that will make you question your motives and goals, and go beyond the dazzle of prizes and awards, beyond the repetition of techniques, and beyond the known—the ultimate goal of the arts.

THE ESSENCE OF OKINAWAN KARATE-DO
by Shoshin Nagamine

> "Nagamine's book will awaken in all who read it a new understanding of the Okinawan open-handed martial art."
> —Gordon Warner
> *Kendo 7th Dan, Renshi*

ESSENTIAL SHORINJIRYU KARATEDO
by Masayuki Kukan Hisataka

> A well-rounded guide to this highly innovative and effective martial art. Describing preset forms, fighting combinations, weapons, and the history and philosophy of Shorinjiryu karate, it is an excellent introduction to this comprehensive modern fighting system.

FILIPINO MARTIAL ARTS: CABALES SERRADA ESCRIMA *by Mark V. Wiley*

> A detailed introduction to this deadly but graceful Filipino art of armed and unarmed combat. Packed full of information on the techniques, tactics, philosophy, spirituality, and history of the Filipino martial arts, this book is a vital addition to any martial arts library.

HEALTH AND FITNESS IN THE MARTIAL ARTS
by Dr. J.C. Canney

> A highly readable, informative, nontechnical text on how to maximize martial arts performance and enhance overall health and fitness. Topics covered include nutrition, the cardiovascular, muscular, and nervous systems, psychology, and training for children.

HSING-I: CHINESE INTERNAL BOXING
by Robert W. Smith and Allen Pittman

A superb introduction to the Chinese art of Hsing-i that both beginners and advanced practitioners can use to probe deeply into the secrets of one of the most complete systems of self-defense yet developed.

JUDO FORMAL TECHNIQUES
by Tadao Otaki and Donn F. Draeger

A comprehensive manual on the basic formal techniques of Kodokan Judo, the *Randori no Kata*, which provide the fundamental training in throwing and grappling that is essential to effective Judo.

THE KARATE DOJO: TRADITIONS AND TALES OF A MARTIAL ARTIST *by Peter Urban*

This book discusses in detail the *dojo*, or training hall. Gives anecdotes on the origins and history of karate, as well as on the important role it has played in history.

KARATE'S HISTORY AND TRADITIONS (REVISED EDITION) *by Bruce A. Haines*

Written by a historian, this book both describes the origins of karate and explains the importance of Zen in the serious study of karate. This authoritative source has been updated to reflect changes that have taken place in the martial arts during the last two decades.

THE NINJA AND THEIR SECRET FIGHTING ART
by Stephen K. Hayes

The ninja were the elusive spies and assassins of feudal Japan. This book explains their lethal system of unarmed combat, unique weapons, and mysterious techniques of stealth.

PA-KUA: EIGHT-TRIGRAM BOXING
by Robert W. Smith and Allen Pittman

This book outlines the history and philosophy of this internal martial art, which is based on the Pa-kua, the eight trigrams of the I-Ching.

SECRET FIGHTING ARTS OF THE WORLD
by John F. Gilbey

Suppressed for centuries, twenty of the world's most secretly guarded fighting techniques are vividly described in this amazing volume.

SECRETS OF SHAOLIN TEMPLE BOXING
edited by Robert W. Smith

" . . . published with the same excellent care and taste that is a feature of all Tuttle books . . . fascinating."
—*The South China Morning Post*

SECRETS OF THE SAMURAI
by Oscar Ratti and Adele Westbrook

"Ratti and Westbrook have captured the breadth and depth of feudal Japanese *bujutsu* and its modern progeny. Anyone with a genuine interest in the roots of Japanese military tradition and martial arts should have this book." —*The Journal of Asian Martial Arts*

SHAOLIN: LOHAN KUNG FU
by P'ng Chye Khim and Donn F. Draeger

A clearly written manual giving detailed explanations of the special elements of South China's Lohan style of Shaolin, including the Lohan pattern in both solo and partner forms.

TAE KWON DO: SECRETS OF KOREAN KARATE
by Sihak Henry Cho

This book teaches Tae Kwon Do, probably the strongest form of self-defense known. This Korean form of karate is highly competitive, and its practice is one of the best ways to achieve mental and physical fitness.

T'AI-CHI: THE "SUPREME ULTIMATE"
EXERCISE *by Cheng Man-ch'ing and Robert W. Smith*

Written by one of the leading Yang-style experts, who studied directly under the legendary Yang Cheng-fu (d. 1935), this book illustrates Cheng's famous short form and includes a translation of the *T'ai-Chi Ch'uan Classics*.

THIS IS KENDO *by Junzo Sasamori and Gordon Warner*

The first book in English to describe the origin and history of kendo, its basic principles and techniques, its etiquette, and its relation to Zen. A must for any serious martial artist.

THE WEAPONS AND FIGHTING ARTS OF INDONESIA *by Donn F. Draeger*

Discover the ancient and modern combative forms of the Indonesian archipelago. As varied as the islands themselves, the styles described in this classic work include mysterious and deadly unarmed and weapons arts.

WING CHUN KUNG-FU: VOLUMES 1, 2, and 3 *by Dr. Joseph W. Smith*

A comprehensive series on this highly effective Chinese martial art. Volume 1 covers the basic forms and principles; Volume 2 illustrates fighting and grappling; and Volume 3 shows weapons and advanced techniques.

ZEN SHAOLIN KARATE: THE COMPLETE PRACTICE, PHILOSOPHY & HISTORY *by Nathan Johnson*

The ultimate interpretation of karate forms. A book that breaks the barriers separating karate, kung fu, and aikido, it revolutionizes the way preset forms are applied in all karate styles.